I BELIEVE

The Personal Structure of Faith

I BELIEVE

The Personal Structure of Faith

by

JEAN MOUROUX

Translated by
Michael Turner

SHEED AND WARD — NEW YORK

NIHIL OBSTAT: Adrianus van Vliet, S.T.D.
Censor deputatus

IMPRIMATUR: E. Morragh Bernard.
Vic. Gen.

Westmonasterii, die 9a Junii, 1959

The Nihil Obstat *and* Imprimatur *are a declaration that a book or pamphlet is considered to be free from doctrinal or moral error. It is not implied that those who have granted the* Nihil Obstat *and* Imprimatur *agree with the contents, opinions or statements expressed.*

I Believe was first published in French, under the title *Je Crois en Toi, structure personelle de la foi*, by Les Editions du Cerf.

Manufactured in the United States of America

Everyone who believes assents to someone's words; and thus, in any form of belief, it seems that it is *the person to whose words the assent is given*, who is of principal importance and, as it were, the end; while the individual truths through which one assents to that person are secondary.

St Thomas Aquinas, *Summa Theologica*
11a 11ae, q.xi, art.1

CONTENTS

PREFACE

A THEOLOGY of faith can be constructed from two distinct points of view. One is analytic and abstract; whether it deals with the origin or the structure of faith, it studies principally its elements: i.e. the subjective factors (intellect, will and grace) or the objective data (credibility, the material object and formal motive). This is the approach usually adopted by theologians. The second is synthetic and concrete; it studies faith as *a concrete whole*, and tries to penetrate its structure as actually given. This is the standpoint generally adopted by Scripture and the Fathers. In our opinion faith can be seen, in this aspect, to be an *organic body of personal relations*.

We believe that this aspect of faith needs particular emphasis in theology. In order to show this, we shall consider faith successively in its objective principles (*testimony*), its subjective movement (*assent*) and also in certain important stages of its development. The arguments we use will be those of classical theology, so rich in its treatment of the subject; they are quite independent, and for good reason, of existentialism

9

as it has developed in this country (France) since 1940. This study gradually took shape as we meditated on Christian personalism and especially on the mystery of the Holy Trinity. The works of St Thomas, which we studied for our purpose, provide abundant material for a much more thorough treatment. But the reader should bear in mind throughout this work the limits of our purpose. We are studying faith as a concrete activity, and emphasising only its personal structure. Even this aspect will be but partially treated, for a person cannot be fully defined apart from his relationships with other human persons. This latter aspect will not be developed systematically in the following pages, for we shall be mainly concerned with the relationship of the human person to God.

I

THE SOURCES OF FAITH
The Personal God

GOD, THE OBJECT AND END
OF FAITH[1]

Credere Deum, credere in Deum, credere Deo: theologians of old were fond of defining faith in terms of this Augustinian formula. In faith God is the object, the end and the witness. In other words, the objective principles of faith are of the personal order. All we have to do is to comment on this formula.

Credere Deum: The first and the essential object of faith is no mere abstract truth, but a personal being—God himself—God as creator and redeemer; God the Father and Jesus Christ whom he has sent; Jesus Christ, Son of God and Saviour; the Spirit, the living promise of the Father and Christ's own gift. In a word, the object of faith is the one God in three Persons, and to have faith is to believe in this personal Being. 'Nobody reaches God's presence until he has learned to

[1] We are using the words *object* and *end* in the sense which they carry in scholastic philosophy, where *object* denotes the term of the activity of knowledge, and *end* the term of the dynamism of the will.

believe that God exists, and that he rewards those who try to find him' (Heb. xi. 6). The whole essence of faith is here: in the divine being are contained all the eternal riches in which our beatitude will one day consist; and in his Providence are contained the temporal organisation of our salvation and all the means—particularly the very person of Christ—by which we may achieve our end.[1] If faith be defined in relation to vision as the power which tends to and prepares us for that vision—*inchoatio vitae aeternae in nobis*—it is necessarily specified by the same object,[2] namely the one God in three persons who is 'believed in' in this life while waiting to be 'known' in the next. 'Eternal life is knowing thee, who art the only true God, and Jesus Christ, whom thou has sent' (John xvii. 3).

Clearly we must interpret literally the classical formula which tells us that 'the object of faith is the First Truth'. Although this formula is in itself quite accurate, it has none the less given rise to

---

[1] 'The divine essence includes all those things which we believe exist in God externally, and in which our beatitude consists; while faith in his providence includes all those things dispensed in time by God for man's salvation, and which are the way to beatitude.' *Summa Theol.*, 11a 11ae, q.i, art.7.

[2] 'The First Truth is the object of vision *in patria*, where it manifests itself in all its brilliance; and it is the object of faith where it remains veiled.' *De Veritate*, XIV, 8, ad.3.

frequent misunderstanding. For us the word 'truth' is abstract, and denotes a relation. The adjective 'first' corrects it, setting this truth on its own, on the absolute level, in the Being in whom intelligence and intelligibility are identified to such an extent that he is truth itself.

There remains the danger that the formula will be understood only at the abstract level, which leads to false perspectives, as though this truth were merely something existing in the mind along with other such mental objects, though more noble than the rest; something serving primarily as a logical rule for this complex operation which is the act of faith. Needless to say, it is nothing of the sort. The first Truth is Subsistent Truth. It is Someone. It is a Person.[1] *God himself under the aspect of First Truth:* this is the explicit and rigorous formula which expresses the object of faith.[2] In the language of theologians, 'God' and 'First Truth' are synonymous,[3] and the second term

[1] In the broad sense of a Personal Being. Cf. *Summa Theol.*, IIIa, q.3, a.3, ad.1.

[2] 'It is God who is the object (of faith) in so far as he is First Truth. . . .' 3 *Sent.*, d.23, 2.1, etc. Cf. *Cajetan:* 'To say that one is united to God as to Truth revealing itself and that one is united to Him in believing in God as God, are two ways of expressing the same reality.' *Commentary* on IIa IIae, I, I, no. 6.

[3] That the two are equivalent is commonly granted: 'The measure and the rule of the theological virtue is God himself: for our faith is regulated according to divine

must always keep the concrete and personal sense which it derives from the first.

As a consequence—and this applies to faith even more than to other kinds of knowledge—the intelligible material—the images, concepts and articles of the Creed—is not the actual object of faith: *actus credentis non terminatur ad enuntiabile, sed ad rem*.[1] All this material is only our way of attaining the luminous object hidden from our gaze; it is the simple object 'cut up', as it were, into separate propositions. These provide the mind with only an inchoate possession of truth, but they lead it on to a full and complete attainment. The perception of faith is, if one may put it this way, a dynamic perception,[2] *perceptio tendens*, and it is this very movement of assent, of affirmation and of desire, which defines the spiritual disposition of the believer. All the 'images, all the created realities which faith uses, are means of

truth.' *Summa Theol.*, 1a 11ae, q.lxiv, a.4. 'If we consider the conclusion to which he assents, he is said to believe in God; for the First Truth is the proper object of faith.' *De Veritate*, XIV, 7, 7.

[1] *Summa Theol.*, 11a 11ae, q.i, a.2, ad.2.

[2] This is the Isidorian expression: '*Articulus est perceptio divinae veritatis, tendens in ipsam.*' Cf. St Thomas, in 3 *Sent.*, d.25, q.1, sol.i, ad.4. Cf. St Bonaventure, 3 *Sent.*, d.24, a.3, q.2: 'The article of faith is at once what gives the mind the light to perceive the divine truth and what stirs up in us the desire of possessing it. . . .'

attaining the unique object'.[1] The First Truth is the object, the end and the cause of faith, and it is to this object that the mind tends through the perception of fragmentary truth.[2] The intellect which is unable to 'see' the object forms a judgment and commits itself to a truth, and *by this very affirmation* tends to the First Truth in itself.[3] Through the affirmations made by my reason I seek and attain being; through the affirmation of faith I seek and attain the Person in whom my beatitude is to be found.

This object is necessarily my end. God is at once the supremely intelligible and the sum of all my desires: faith is a *credere in Deum*. To be absolutely precise, God as First Truth is the object of faith, and as Supreme Good he is the end of faith.[4] But because First Truth signifies both the necessary being and the adorable Person, we must say, without drawing distinctions, that the First Truth is the proper end of the will.[5] The two

[1] 'The images by which faith perceives something are not themselves the object of faith, but the means by which faith reaches its object.' *De Veritate*, q.14, a.8, ad.11.

[2] 3 *Sent.*, d.25, a.1, q.1, sol.4.

[3] 'The assent of faith, by which we judge a complex proposition to be true, tends towards the First Truth as its object; and therefore there is no reason why the First Truth should not be the object of faith, although it is expressed in many propositions.' *De Veritate*, XIV, 8, 5.

[4] 3 *Sent.*, d.23, q.2, a.1.

[5] 'The First Truth itself stands in relation to the act of

aspects are in no way separable, particularly as
they are always affirmed as bound up with one
another in the inseparable unity of one single act:
I tend towards God as First Truth because I tend
to him as the source of beatitude. The God who
is seen by St John as the 'God of Truth' and the
God who is seen by St Paul as the 'Author of
Beatitude' is one. In the same way, there are no
truths of faith except in relation to God as First
Truth and to God as the author of Beatitude. The
more essential an article of faith, the more it is
identified with the very Being of God; and equally,
the more essential it is, the more it will be linked
with our ultimate happiness, with our beatitude.
All this is strongly brought out by St Thomas: the
truths which order us directly to eternal life, in
the vision of which we are blessed, belong *of themselves* to faith, in short: 'fidei objectum per se est
id per quod homo beatus efficitur'.[1]

Once again there is no question of separate items
of belief; the object of faith is at once Truth and
Beatitude. To be more precise, the object of faith
is that Personal Being who is at once Truth and

---

faith as its end inasmuch as it is something invisible to us.'
11a 11ae, q.4, a.1. 'Because, as St Augustine shows, the First
Truth which is the object of faith is the end of all our
desires and actions.' *Summa Theol.*, 11a 11ae, q.ii, a.2
and q.iv, a.2, ad.3.

[1] *Ibid.*, 11a 11ae, q.i, a.6, ad.1; a.8 and q.ii, a.5.

Beatitude.[1] That is why the act of faith is both an affirmation and an act of love—a love which desires a Person, and which affirms that Person in order to possess Him.

FAITH, THE TESTIMONY OF GOD

GOD is not only the object and the end of faith; he is also its witness, and the act of faith must always be *credere Deo*.

It is because God speaks to me that I believe. The personal rôle played by God should be more strongly in evidence here than before; the reason I believe is that God bears witness to himself, and by this means calls me to faith and to salvation: 'No one can come to me unless the Father who sent me should draw him'—but what exactly is this 'drawing'?

It is, first, an *interior vocation* to faith. This vocation is the essential and proper characteristic of the divine testimony, not only because the Divine Being can penetrate where the human being cannot, because the Absolute Spirit can penetrate

[1] 'The Uncreated Being is the object of faith under the aspect of truth. In so far as it arouses desire it reveals itself as good, and this explains the dynamism of faith towards it. . . .' *De Caritate* 3, c. Cf. Cajetan, *Commentary* on 11a 11ae, 5,1, n 5: 'Faith has as its first object the Triune God who constitutes our supernatural beatitude. . . .'

to the very core of the created spirit; but especially because between God and each individual soul there exists a personal relation which is the relationship of vocation. God made each soul for himself, so that it might glorify him and bear the fruit of its freedom in re-joining him.

God alone knows man's eternal name, his name of grace which will not be revealed in this life, but which is, none the less, his most profound reality. When God calls a soul it is this name which, in some mysterious way, he lets him hear, and for this reason he speaks always to the innermost depths of the soul.

God, then, works within man, and the soul in its innermost depths experiences his action, which is both illumination and inspiration, a summons of light and love. At this stage we must give back their real, realistic sense to the usual formulas. We say: it is grace which enlightens and attracts—and this is perfectly true; but it means that *God himself*, in his personal reality, enlightens and attracts us by his grace. It is not the action of a blind force, an impassive sun shedding light without discrimination. It is a Person, who is light and love, who gives a little of himself to a person in need, one who craves that light and love. If God as Creator attracts a human being through that instinct in man which is the natural desire of his spirit, how much more intimately does God as Person attract and call me through the new desire which he himself instils in me—*interiori instinctu Dei invitantis*.[1] God himself, by virtue of his grace, prepares me to believe.[2] In the end it is God who will have brought me by his grace to the act of assent.[3] It must be said, in strict accuracy: 'It is God who causes faith in the believer by prompting his will and enlightening his intellect.'[4]

In this, moreover, lies the ultimate explanation of that leap into another world, which is faith. Man does not take this leap by himself, and consequently he does not act against his reason; he crosses the gulf, and transcends the limits of his reason, through his reliance on his guide—*altiori dirigenti*

[1] *Summa Theol.*, IIa IIae, q.ii, a.9, ad.3. Cf. *In Ioannem* c.vi, lect.5, no. 3: 'But because it is not only exterior or objective revelation which has a power of attraction, but also the interior instinct impelling and moving men to belief, therefore the Father draws many to the Son by the interior instinct of the divine operation moving the heart of man to believe. . . .'

[2] 'Belief depends on the will of the believer; but man's will needs to be prepared by God through grace, so that it may be raised to things which are above nature.' *Summa Theol.*, IIa IIae, q.vi, a.1, ad.3.

[3] 'Faith, as regards this assent which is its principal act, comes from God who moves us inwardly by his grace.' *Ibid.*, IIa IIae, q.vi, a.1.

[4] *De Veritate*, XXV, 11, 8, 12.

innixus.[1] Man takes the hand held out to help him, he knows that he is not throwing himself into a void, but into arms which are ready to close round him in welcome.[2] And because each human being is a sinner, this call is at once a call to renunciation and to giving. A call tender, intimate and particularised, never the same for any two souls, even when they are moved by the same word or sign, since it is always a question of the Personal God attracting an individual soul to himself. The grace given by God is at once personal and personalising; *personal*, because it is directed to an individual soul in its own determined situation, *personalising*, because it is destined to make the individual soul realise its own unique vocation. Grace is only a means; God alone is the agent.

Normally, however, the mode of God's testimony is in accord with the actual psychology of the individual human, and so we can say in the strict sense of the words that *God speaks.* God himself tells me the truths of faith, through human

[1] 'A believer is not someone who denies his reason by acting against it; rather, he goes beyond it, through being guided by a light of a higher order, namely the First Truth.' 3 *Sent.*, d.24.

[2] 'All men need to be drawn. God, in so far as it depends on him, lends his hand to all men to draw them to him; still more, he not only takes the hand of those ready to receive him, but even turns towards him those who have turned away.' *In Ioannem*, c.vi, lect.5, no. 3.

lips.[1] The first witness was God made man, the
Word made flesh. The second witness, perpetuat-
ing and representing the first among men, is the
Church. There is an ontological and an organic
unity between the two, the unity of body and
Head. For this reason the process is identical in
both cases. God spoke to the Jews through the
historical Christ, and until the end of time he
speaks to mankind by means of the *Mystical*
Christ. Here we come across a formula which
presents a serious problem: 'God's word is a
human word.' In so far as the human word has
not been comprehended for what it really is—the
word of God—the testimony of God remains unknown and faith is not attained. The word of
God, as a rule, is God speaking to me through a
man, and this word is itself a grace—*gratia
locutionis*.[2] Just as God works inwardly in the

[1] 'The believer gives his assent to a man not in so far as
he is a man, but in so far as God is making use of him to
transmit his word, and this can easily be verified by certain
indications.' 3 *Sent.*, d.23, q.2, a.2, sol.2, ad.3. 'Neither the
testimony of a man nor that of an angel leads us to assent
infallibly to the truth, except in so far as, through them, we
are brought into contact with the testimony of God revealing
himself.' *De Veritate*, q.xiv, a.8. 'To some they are revealed
by God immediately, as was the case with the Apostles and
prophets; while to others they are proposed by God in
sending preachers of the faith.' *Summa Theol.*, iia iiae,
q.vi, a.i.

[2] *Contra Gent.*, iii, 154.

human soul through his grace, so he reaches the intellect and will by his Revealed Word, his astonishing and scandalising word, which yet springs from love. It is by no means a dead word, but 'living and long-enduring', effectual and transforming, a word sharper than any sword, opening up mysterious wounds by which life enters into a being hitherto shut in on itself; because this is the Living Word of the Living God, directed to a particular living soul, to bring it to Him.[1]

This word, sown by Christ and the Apostles, is transmitted to the Church by the voice of the Pope and the Bishops. The voice of the liturgy brings it ever anew to attentive souls, though too often its sound is remote. The voice of the priest distributes it to the faithful, applying, adapting and fitting it to particular circumstances. The voice of genuine Christians lets it be heard in those pagan regions which comprise to an enormous extent the societies and individual souls of today. Sometimes even, God may whisper it directly to a soul.[1] By all these ways, at different times and in different manners, it is truly God's own word which is transmitted; it is the word of Jesus Christ

[1] In this case there is an *auditus interior*. Early writers were not so reticent as we are on this point; cf. St Thomas: faith is *ex auditu* 'because the determination of what is to be believed comes about in us by means of the interior word by which God speaks to us, or else by the exterior word'. 3 *Sent.*,

which is prolonged, it is God who speaks to the souls of today.

Consequently there is no call for astonishment at the miracles which this word accomplishes; for it also is a grace of God, it is 'spirit and life'. The formal motive of faith, in the strict sense of the term, is the testimony of God who is the First Truth, and of God who uses the human voice to speak to me—the voice of Christ and of his Church. The contact between Christ and God is direct: 'What I tell the world is only what I have learned from him who sent me, because he cannot deceive' (John viii. 26). Because Christ is a Divine Person, this learning must take place within God himself, and is at the same time a vision.

'We speak of what is known to us, and testify of what our eyes have seen' (John iii. 11). Through Christ, our connection with God is assured. The witness transmits what he knows of the Word Incarnate: 'Our message concerns that Word, who is life; what he was from the first, what we have heard about him, what our own eyes have seen of him; what it was that met our gaze, and the touch of our hands . . . and it is as eyewitnesses

---

d.23, q.3, a.2, ad.2; and St Bonaventure, *ibid* d.24,. dub.2, concludes thus: 'When the Apostle says in a general manner that faith is born from preaching, we must interpret this more of that preaching which is heard by the interior soul than of that which sounds in the exterior ears.'

that we give you news of that life, that eternal life' (1 John i. 1); and God manifests his word in him: 'and now, in due time, he had made his meaning clear to us, through the preaching with which God, our Saviour, has seen fit to entrust me' (Titus i. 3). What is true of the apostles who were the first witnesses is true of the Church which is the permanent witness. Consequently; 'The formal object of divine faith is the First Truth as it is manifested in *Holy Scripture and the teaching of the Church*, which teaching takes its origin from the First Truth.'[1] No matter what the human intermediaries may be, it is the living and personal Word of God which presents the truths of faith to the soul until the end of time.

The same holds for the signs by which God accredits his testimony. They are not, essentially, general proofs, abstract causes of conviction, principles for technical demonstration. They can, and should, function as such, but they are not primarily of this order. They are interventions of God, signs, calls, whether imperious or unobtrusive, sudden like a flash of lightning or tranquil as a stream, but always directed by God to a soul, or to a group of souls (and within the

[1] This is a traditional thesis in spite of the neglect which it has suffered for so long. Several texts of (scholastic) theologians on this point may be found in Marin Sola: *L'Evolution homogène du Dogme Catholique* (Gabalda, 1924), vol. 1, pp. 218–28.

group to each one personally). This is inevitable:
if God speaks to me now, he also gives me a sign
now.

These signs are in origin personal, primarily
because they form part of God's testimony. They
are not an additional element, added on from
outside, nor are they proofs connected with the
divine message and object just by some extrinsic
statement or process of reasoning. They are manifestations of a real presence, they demonstrate
that the Personal God is acting. Reasons cannot
deduce the datum of faith from its principles,
because this datum transcends reason; nor can
reason demonstrate it, because it is not implicit in
the primary material from which reason works.

That is why God gives us signs which demonstrate clearly that the word comes from him.[1]
Thenceforth it is a matter of understanding,
reading and interpreting these signs correctly.
The rôle of the intellect will consist in grasping
a concrete meaning,[2] for signs cannot be the first

[1] 'The preaching of the faith could not receive confirmation (of its truth) *by demonstration* and through rational
principles, since the truths of the faith are above reason.
So it was fitting that the words of the preachers of the faith
should be confirmed by signs clearly indicating that their
preaching came from God. . . .' *Contra Gent.*, III, 154.

[2] 'If men are allowed to work miracles, this is in order
to show that God is speaking through them.' 3 *Sent.*, d.25,
q.2, a.1, sol.4, ad.4.

principles in a deduction, but they are facts bearing a significance; *facta divinâ, signa certissima.* We must go further: these signs make one with the witness himself. With Christ, the signs are sometimes his person, sometimes his doctrine or his acts—the doctrine and the acts being manifestations of the very person of Christ who is simultaneously the witness and the object of faith. With the Church, the signs are the marks of this 'mysterious person' of whom Christ is the head and men are the members: these signs—holiness, catholicity, fruitfulness and unity—are all manifestations of that Church which is, again, at once the witness and the object of faith. It is by means of these signs that the personal God reveals himself and makes himself recognised. 'The finger of God is there'.

Personal in their origin, these signs are invariably directed to a person. God neither acts nor speaks to men in general. God does not address himself to creatures in the general and the abstract. He speaks to each soul in its innermost and most personal depths, as we have already seen. It follows that the miracle worked before a crowd is not addressed to that crowd as such, but to each individual who goes to make up the crowd. It speaks to the eye, while grace speaks to the heart, and it is from the meeting of these two elements of testimony—the exterior sign and the interior grace—that the act of faith will spring.[1] But these two elements arise from one single action of the same God, and are merely two ways which the divine Person uses to contact the human soul, and to awaken it to its vocation, which is faith. It is a double entreaty, to which man will respond with an *élan* of his whole being, or which, on the other hand, he will use his liberty to refuse.

From this point of view, we can explain a number of the real motives of conversion, which seem, at first, to do violence to reason. It is not necessary here to enter into a controversy which has been so hotly debated by theologians.[2] But if we mark that the motives of credibility are signs addressed personally by God to a human person,

---

[1] *Summa Theol.*, 11a 11ae, q.vi, a.1: 'It is clear that Christ drew men to himself by his words and by signs both visible and invisible, that is by moving and stirring their inward hearts; . . . Therefore, the words of Our Lord, "If I had not done these works . . ." are to be understood not only of his visible works but equally of this interior attraction of his teaching . . .' (*In Ioannem*, cap XV, lect.5, n.4). Cf. St Bonaventure: 'Although the apostles learnt many things by seeing Christ, they learnt much more through hearing him, who spoke to them exteriorly, and interiorly, too, by the Holy Spirit.' 3 *Sent.*, d.24, dub.2.

[2] Certain theologians demand, for motives of credibility which are anterior to faith, the greatest possible objectivity and logical strictness; others say that the importance of these motives in the act of faith is relative, and that rigorously objective proofs established without any help from grace are

we will realise that their value, i.e. their meaning, lies primarily in the fact that they have been chosen and used by God. The forms which they take, the elements which seem fleeting, slight, even ephemeral in the eyes of a cold and impersonal critic, are of little importance. What matters is their significance, their spirit, the meaning they hold, the presence they actually manifest. From the moment God invests them with meaning they are fully and objectively valid, as valid as other motives which can be collated and presented technically. They differ from these others in communicability, not in their solidity. This, which to some seems alarming, is only to be expected once we have understood that these signs are all part of a personal and concrete approach by God. Since the truth is communicated by the Church to men in general, and since the Church has to bear convincing witness both to the ordinary seeker after God and to the more exacting, there are and always will be in Catholicism signs and collections of signs which can be built up into technical demonstrations or made to serve as rational proofs. But, because assent to truth is a personal and unique process, there are and there

---

merely illusions. A detailed and interesting study of the controversy can be found in R. Aubert, *Le Problème de l'acte de foi: données traditionelles et résultats des controverses récentes*, Louvain, 1945.

always will be signs whose origin lies in the life of the individual; they are sometimes purely interior, sometimes exterior but rationally very weak, and even, at times, 'scandalous' to the outside observer. *From the theological point of view* this makes little difference, for in these cases it is always God in whom the soul believes.

So far we have been considering mainly converts, but all this applies to ordinary, uneducated persons, provided that they really are Christians. They also have their signs, and excellent ones at that; they can be systematically arranged by a careful apologist, and so brought out to full awareness.[1] But these signs, or rather this unique sign, made up of all the converging elements of one life, culminates in the manifestation of a presence —the presence of *my* God within the very structure

[1] The theologians of the Vatican Council noted this: 'Although the uninstructed faithful (*rudiores*) have no distinct knowledge of all the motives of credibility and cannot explain them, they do none the less, in their own manner, know the Church as one, holy, catholic and apostolic, and in this Church there is always present before their eyes a motive of credibility, or rather a complexus of motives, which is unchangeable, quite sufficient and certain; so that they do not believe lightly, as do unthinking souls, but so that they rest on secure foundations in view of the full certitude of credibility, being always ready (as all must be according to their condition) to satisfy—through and in the Church—the demands and questions of those who ask of them the reason for the hope which is theirs, etc.' *Acta Concilii Vaticani, collectio Lacensis, 533.*

of *my* existence. This sign sometimes provides elements which are easily built into a synthesis, but sometimes it practically defies any rational systematisation. But then it defies rationalisation no more than all those signs which in everyday life show us the presence, loyalty and love of a human person. Once again we have here a sign which is less amenable than others to communication, but not less real, since it lets the soul recognise with the living certainty of personal intuition the presence in its life of the God of Truth and happiness.[1]

To be strictly accurate we must say that, in faith, it is really *God who invites us*. Through grace, through words, through signs, in an infinite variety of ways, the Personal God calls the human being to give itself to him by faith, and, by responding to its vocation, to realise completely its spiritual personality. 'God so loved the world, that he gave up his only-begotten Son, so that those who believe in him . . . may have eternal life' (John iii. 16).

---

[1] 'God is always causing man's justification, even as the sun is always lighting up the air. Hence grace is not less effective when it comes to a believer than when it comes to someone who does not believe; since it causes faith in both, *in the former by confirming and perfecting it*, in the latter by creating it anew.' *Summa Theol.*, 11a 11ae, q.iv, a.4, ad.3. The soul perceives the *result* of this divine action in which man collaborates.

FAITH, A REALITY IN CHRIST

'. . . so that those who believe in him may have eternal life' (John iii. 16). These words point to the most real and personal characteristic of faith, considered objectively. Our faith is Christian and it is defined entirely in relation to Christ. 'I am the Way, the Truth and the Life.' Christ is *the way*, but he is also the object and the end. The way, because of this human nature he has taken, which makes of him the man 'who tells you the truth as I have heard it from God' (John viii. 40). The way also, and much more profoundly so, through his divine person itself, which is a pure subsistent relation to the Father and the Holy Spirit, and which is One with them in the possession of the same divine nature. Because he and the Father (and the Spirit) are one, to know him is to know the Father; to see and to love him is to see and to love the Father; to possess him is to possess the Father, and the Spirit who springs forth from their love. So that to believe in him is to believe in the Father and the Holy Spirit, and so to possess eternal life.[1]

[1] 'The learning which I impart is not my own, it comes from him who sent me' (John vii. 16). St Augustine comments: 'You must understand that Christ, the Son of God, *who is the doctrine of the Father* (this is the personal aspect) does not possess his origin within himself, but is the *Son of*

Thus our faith is Christological and, because of this, it is also Trinitarian. These two affirmations are not opposed, they are implied in each other. In Christ we attain the whole Trinity; and it is only in Christ that we attain it. 'In order to go to God it is first necessary to believe that he exists': this is verified to the letter in Christ. In Christ, and in him alone, we find the one God in three Persons. Because the whole order of providence is contained in the Son, we should extend this formula and add 'And he *rewards* those who seek him'. Christ is the sole Redeemer, he is the living propitiation. The Father has given into his hands everything in the sphere of Redemption. Eternally He gives being to the Word; in the same way, and in consequence, he sent the Incarnate Word to bring his testimony to men; to have life in himself, to possess the Holy Spirit in its fullness, and to communicate it to his own.

---

the Father (this is the Trinitarian aspect).' *In Ioannem*, Tr. XXX, 6; P.L., XXXV, 1631. Augustine, who suggested to St Thomas the difference between *credere Deum, Deo, in Deum*, teaches the same doctrine in regard to Christ when he explains the 'credere Christum, et in Christum' (e.g. S. de Verb. Dom. 164, 2, 2; P.L., XXXVIII, 788); and the 'credere Christo et in Christum' (e.g. *In Ioannem*, XXIX, 6; P.L., XXXV, 1631). Cf. Th. Camelot, *Credere Deo, credere Deum, credere in Deum. Pour l'histoire d'une formule traditionelle.* (Les Sciences philosophiques et théologiques, 1941–42, pp. 149–56.)

All the Father's promises are fulfilled in Jesus Christ, and he is the living 'amen' in whom the Father gives himself to men. Hence the aphorisms of the primitive Christians: 'It is only through the Holy Spirit that anyone can say, Jesus is the Lord' (1 Cor. xii. 3). 'What he commands is that we should have faith in the name of his Son Jesus Christ' (1 John iii. 23). These formulas contain the whole of the faith in so far as being Christological they are necessarily Trinitarian: 'united in the same Spirit, we have access through him to the Father' (Eph. ii. 18). And so, 'he who possesses the Christian faith *rightly*, assents with his will to Christ in whatever is truly part of Christ's teaching'.[1] There is nothing vague about such a doctrine. The object of Christian faith is that Truth which in fact is the Person who is God. To say 'the Truth' is the same as to say 'the Incarnate Son', and Our Lord stressed this equality when he told us that to be made free by the truth is to be made free by the Son: 'If you continue faithful to my word, you are my disciples in earnest; so you will come to know the truth, *and the truth will set you free. . . . If it is the Son who makes you free men*, you will have freedom in earnest' (John viii. 32, 36).

We do not need to insist that Christ is the witness of faith, *testis verus et fidelis*, the true and faithful

[1] *Summa Theol.*, 11a 11ae, q.xi, a.1.

witness (Apoc. 3, 14); or that he speaks, works miracles, draws men to him by grace, and bears a witness which is identical with that of God himself. The testimony he gives in such abundance is certainly his own, yet the words he uses are not 'his' words, but the Father's; his works not 'his', but the Father's; his life not 'his', but the Father's. Here, once again, he who calls us is Christ, and through him the Father and the whole Trinity. 'None knows the Father truly except the Son, and those to whom it is the Son's good pleasure to reveal him' (Matt. xi. 27). 'Nobody can come to the Father, except through me' (John xiv. 6): *and at the same time*, 'Nobody can come to me without being attracted towards me by the Father who sent me' (John vi. 44).[1] The word of God is the word of Christ; God's works are Christ's works; God's grace is Christ's grace; the testimony of God is the testimony of Christ; they are all one[2] because Christ and the Father are one. The grace of testimony is also Christological, and conse-

[1] St Thomas: 'Thus the faithful are drawn by the Father, enticed by his majesty, but they are drawn equally by the Son, drawn towards him by a wonderful feeling of delight and by the love of that truth which is the Son of God himself.' *In Ioannem*, CVI, lect.5, n.3.

[2] 'The knowledge which we have of the Father we have received from him who has seen him—the Son; no-one can know the Father unless Christ reveals him; and in the same way no-one can come to the Son unless he has received the manifestation of the Son from the Father.' *Ibid.*, n.5, end.

quently Trinitarian: *Fides Christi, id est, fides gratiae christianae.*[1]

Christian Faith is specified in its entirety by Christ; it is participation in the life of a person,[2] in the mystery of his death and resurrection; thanks to this mediation it is ·a trinitarian faith, and a sharing in the life of the Three Persons. It could not be otherwise, since its object is Christ in whom we find the Three Persons; its source is the grace of Christ, in whom the 'Author of Beatitude', the Triune God, gives and reveals himself. We can now affirm in a much deeper sense that the grace of faith is a personal grace. God is indeed the object, end and witness of faith; this formula is correct. But we now see it to mean that the object, the end and the witness of faith is God, Father, Son and Holy Spirit, revealed in Christ. Faith, then, objectively considered, is the call of the One God in Three Persons, through Christ, to a human person.[3]

[1] St Augustine, *De fide et op.*, XVI, 27 (P.L., XL, 215).

[2] Cf. the important commentary by Bonsirven, *'Les Epitres de Saint Jean'* (Beauchesne, coll. Verbum Salutis, 1936) on 1 John ii. 5–6: 'Every difficulty is resolved if we refer our relationships of indwelling in God to that relationship which is their type and principle, namely the indwelling or circumincession of the Persons in the Holy Trinity', etc.

[3] (Culpable) unbelievers are 'those who have not received the God and Father who called them by the Incarnate Son'. St Maximus the Confessor, *Quest. 60 ad Thal* (P.G., XC, 637 c.).

II

THE HEART OF FAITH
The Response of Free Men

FAITH, A PERSONAL ACT

It follows that faith is, of its essence, the response of the human person to the Personal God, and thus it is *the meeting of two persons*. In the act of faith the *whole* man is involved, and this explains some of the essential characteristics of faith. In the first place the act of faith is at one and the same time both a simple act and a concrete whole—it might be called a complex, if we can leave aside the usual connotations of that word.[1]

We can never stress sufficiently that this act which has so many different elements is a *simple act*. Where life is concerned, simplicity comes first, and complexity is the outcome of critical analysis —albeit a legitimate outcome.[2]

[1] We are aware that philosophers are widening the meaning of this word more and more; cf. Spaier, in *Recherches Philosophiques* (IV, 1934, p. 1 et seq.); H. Gouhier, in *Études carmélitaines* (April 1937, p. 231): 'In this aspect there is a religious psychology of the reason: the Christian thinker's way of understanding is a special complex'; Yves de Montcheuil, *Recherches de Science Religieuse* (1937, pp. 130–31).

[2] In *Les mécanismes du cerveau* (Gallimard, Paris, 1938, p. 109), J. Lhermitte writes: 'To believe, says Goldstein, that a purely analytic method simplifies things is an error, for simplicity does not reside in the so-called element of classical

So it is with faith—it is a simple act, because it
is the gift of the whole man.[1] Analysis will show
therein the presence of will, of thought and
spiritual feelings, but all this is within the unity
of one vital act,[2] the act of a person who unites
himself with another person. Since the object of
faith is not on the one hand truth, and on the
other happiness, but a person who is both truth
and happiness, the human being does not *first* have
to grasp truth and then wait to be drawn to this
happiness; he has simply to unite himself in one

---

biology, but in the vital system considered as a whole. The
reflexes, which are elementary phenomena, express merely a
reaction of the organism of which certain parts are isolated;
and only an abstraction or an amputation obtained by
experiment or illness can realise this isolation.'

[1] The unformed act of faith is not, despite appearances,
simpler than the act of faith informed by charity. It is an
act *imperfect in itself*, internally deficient, which can be
understood only by comparison with the full and direct
act of faith informed by charity. The analysis of this
unformed faith is obviously useful since this unformed faith
remains a wonderful grace given by God to a sinner. On
the other hand, it is really only the analysis of an abnormal
state of faith, a mutilated act, the act of a dead faith which
is ineffective for salvation. We must take these considera-
tions into account when we try to analyse faith in its real
fullness.

[2] 'These three do not designate three different acts of
faith, but one and the same act which has different relations
with the object of faith.' *Summa Theol.*, 11a 11ae, q.ii, a.2,
ad.3. On the actual movement of faith, cf. the famous
augustinian text of 3 *Sent.*, d.23, q.2, a.2, ad.5.

single movement to the Adorable Person who will beatify him.[1] Consequently, in the act of faith, love must penetrate and direct knowledge.

We cannot come into real contact with a person by the use of our critical faculty, by the sort of reasoning that we use to resolve problems; still less can we reach him by acts proceeding from blind impulse or animal appetite. A person is apprehended in *a spiritual contact* and by a *phenomenon of communion*. The degree of apprehension may vary enormously, and this holds good too of faith itself, whether it be unformed faith or faith informed by charity. But if the persons meet each other then there will always be this phenomenon of communion; and, in the case of living faith, the whole spiritual being throws itself open to welcome the God who calls it. In this way we can see how it is that love is the gateway to faith. We can see above all that love and knowledge are *inseparable* in this act, because both are essential activities of the human person, and because in this case the human person is giving himself to his God. In other words, it is the human being as a unity which is given, for it is neither the will nor the intellect which exists but the man, and it is this

[1] 'Although elements pertaining to the will can be considered accidental to the acts of the intellect, they are however *essential to faith:* just as rational elements which are accidental to sense-appetite are nevertheless essential to the virtue of temperance.' *De Veritate*, q.XIV, a.3, ad.10.

wholeness which is at work in faith, finding fulfil-
ment in giving itself, or else mutilation in refusing
to make this gift.[1]

The very depth of this simple act causes it to
contain a multiplicity of elements. St Thomas was
well aware of the reality of this 'complex', and it
is this notion which enables us to give their full
sense to those curious and profound formulae
by which he expresses this simple movement
which involves all our spiritual powers—this
entire commitment of our whole being as a single
unity. When he emphasises that the assent of faith
takes place under the command of the will, or
according as the will determines the intellect,[2]
these affirmations imply, if they are to be intelligible, the natural unity of the intellect and

[1] We can find yet another proof in the way in which St
Thomas replies to the question, 'Is it necessary for salvation
to believe anything which surpasses natural reason?' *Summa
Theol.*, IIa IIae, q.ii, a.3. Reply: Human nature is not at
the summit of being, but only at a certain level; therefore
it is organically dependent upon a superior nature; it is a
spiritual nature, and so immediately ordered to God
(*dependence upon* and *being ordered to* correspond to one another).
This means: 1. The person is orientated to some further end
and receptive just as much as he is subsistent and complete
(because he *subsists* in *a* nature): 2. He is naturally receptive
to a 'supernatural participation in the divine goodness'.
3. Where faith is concerned it is his natural desire as a
spiritual person which is involved, and which God comes
to fulfil.

[2] *Summa Theol.*, IIa IIae, q.ii, a.9, and q.xi, a.1, ad.3.

THE HEART OF FAITH

the will. Having in mind all purely rational certitudes, he writes even more significantly: 'The intellect gives its assent to the object . . . by inclining voluntarily, by some sort of choice, to one side or the other.' [1] Now, the intellect does not itself choose, but what St Thomas means is that this simple movement, in which choice gives birth to assent, takes place within the mind.

In this vital process, desire and love are involved to such a degree that it is actually their object which the intellect grasps: 'It is by faith that the mind perceives what it hopes for and what it loves.' [2] St Thomas has constructed the theory of this complex in passages of great profundity, which are all too little known.

In man the spiritual powers are organically connected. Although these powers are diverse and irreducible,[3] they are arranged and ordered in relation to one another. Since they are within an 'order', they take on a special value when they develop according to that order; by their reciprocal connections they lead to the formation of those concrete wholes which we call virtues. All this is clear from the following simple statement: 'The act of concupiscence is praiseworthy

[1] *Ibid.*, 11a 11ae, q.i, a.4.

[2] *Ibid.*, 11a 11ae, q.lxii, a.4.

[3] Freud, we realise, would insist on the *pluralism* of the human being; cf. R. Dalbiez, *La Methode psychanalytique et la Doctrine freudienne* (Desclée de Brouwer, 1936), 11, 114 et seq.

in so far as it is in harmony with the reason; the act of reason, in so far as it is in harmony with the intellect that rules it; and the acts of the superior powers, according to the harmony which they have with the end.'[1] Hence we have the following definition of moral virtue: 'Looked at in the right way, the virtue of the appetitive powers is nothing but a disposition, or a form, "sealed" and inserted into the appetite by the reason.'[2]

Faith is a particular case of a concrete totality, but realised on a higher and more mysterious plane than the rest, and that is why St Thomas writes: 'Faith is in the speculative intellect as subject to the will, in the *same way* as temperance is in the appetite subject to reason.'[3] To put this in modern terms: chastity is a complex; and in its own way faith is equally a complex. Knowledge and love in faith are not realities which are brought together from outside, but powers which are produced from within, because they convey an impulse which is more profound than they are. They find their unity in the act of faith, because this act itself manifests the movement of a personal inwardness, a concrete and subsistent unity. The act of faith is the *gift of himself* which the created person makes to the Uncreated Being;

[1] 3 *Sent.*, d.24, a.3, sol.2.
[2] *De Virtut. in Comm.*, 9, c.end; cf. *ibid.*, 10, ad.15.
[3] *Ibid.*, 7.c.

thus it is knowledge which is brought about by love.[1] We must not seek the unity of this act on the level of knowledge and love; it must be sought at that deeper level at which knowledge and love are identified in the spiritual impulse of the person himself.

This explains how the normal and the conscious elements of the act can be found provisionally separate from each other and from the spiritual power which normally would join them into a single whole. This is the case whenever there is a violent change in the orientation of the person, in many cases of conversion for example. The transition from unbelief is in fact a disintegration and a reconstruction.

It is the disintegration of a first complex, which has its roots in the being, is organised around a human centre (most often around the 'self'), is carried along by love, makes up the person's spiritual universe and determines the direction of his life. With the act of faith this disintegrates, because its centre and source are changed, and another complex is built up whose centre is God.[2]

[1] St Thomas constantly affirms that faith inclines to assent *in the manner of* the moral virtues: desire and a minimum of inner rectitude are intrinsic to knowledge by faith, and they define one of the essential features of the act.

[2] This psychology of conversion has been described with considerable insight by R. Guardini in *Vom Leben des Glaubens*, Chapter 1.

It is not only his cherished ideas that are upset, but the meaning of his thoughts, the coherence of his affirmations, the whole inner balance of his spiritual life are transformed. The change is not principally at the level of the conscious elements of this life, but at the level of the spiritual attitude controlling, fostering and organising those elements.

Hence comes the crucifying aspect of conversion: the person, who always recognises by what he possesses, and who always partially identifies himself with this possession, has a painful (and quite correct) feeling that he must lose himself in order to save himself. We can even find cases where the conscious elements of the life of unbelief preserve a stability and organisation which, although only partial, are none the less very real. The convert will then experience a dissociation between the spiritual centre which has been transformed and the conscious surface which quietly persists; he is torn apart by this feeling of a personality which has been radically changed, while his store of ideas, judgments and desires remains completely intact. One, out of many such cases, was Claudel.[1] This state, though certainly ab-

[1] 'My philosophical convictions were complete. God had graciously left them where they were; I saw nothing there to change; the Catholic religion still seemed to me the same treasury of absurd stories, its priests and faithful inspired

normal, is very significant. The spiritual impetus which is faith—the minute seed destined to become the mighty tree—has, little by little, to fight its way and establish a lodging in the soul, despite all that burdens it. Victory would be impossible, were not the entire person engaged in this spiritual movement, engaged on the work of construction and completion, adhering whole-heartedly to the God who calls him in order to save him.

FAITH, A PERSONAL CONTACT

IF this personal point of view throws light on the origin of the act of faith, it can also throw light on its properties. We shall show how it does so in the case of obscurity and of certitude.

The act of faith is obscure, firstly because it is self-revelation by one person to another, and this is always obscure to the discursive reason. The task of the latter is to understand by establishing

in me that same aversion, which went as far as hatred and disgust. The edifice of my opinions and my knowledge remained intact and I saw no fault in them. It was simply that I had left them. A new and formidable being had revealed itself, making frightening demands upon the young man and artist that I was, and I did not know how to reconcile this with anything which surrounded me. The state of a man who has suddenly been torn out of his own flesh to be placed in a strange body in the middle of an unknown world. . . .'

relations and constructing its object. In so doing it works in the light, even though it may not be completely clear to itself, because it relies upon evidence which it cannot analyse, and upon principles which it cannot build up itself.[1] But obscurity to the reason is characteristic of all forms of concrete knowledge, and especially when it is a question of knowledge of persons.

The knowledge of a spiritual person is not discursive; consciousness cannot be constructed from the outside; a person does not come upon himself at the end of a series of abstract relations. The discursive function of the intellect can certainly prepare for, but cannot accomplish this grasping of a concrete existence. It cannot bring about this phenomenon of interpretation *en bloc* which is the discovery of a person similar to the 'self', still less can it enter into the privacy of this spiritual person who is both unique and 'social'.[2]

Even supposing that the 'spiritual core' of a

[1] Cf. G. Rabeau, *Réalité et relativité* (Vrin, 1927), p. 227, '. . . this evidence which is deceptive and humiliating for man's reason, in that what is understood is only understood by that which is not understood in the proper sense. . . .'

[2] This is why a pure rationalism is led to deny the personal existence of other consciousnesses, and to make of the consciousness of another 'a piece in the system of its judgments of existence'. Thus L. Brunschvicg replying to M. Bresson at the *Société française de Philosophie* (1921). Quoted in Etcheverry, *L'Idéalisme française contemporaine* (Alcan, 1934), p. 223.

being could reveal itself to another as Scheler wished, this would still be on a non-discursive level;[1] the existence and value of the person escape this function of the intellect—they are 'obscure' to it. Further we must recognise that this perception is not the luminous penetration of an inner reality. It is much more a global grasping of a spiritual existence, a sort of *contact* and *co-incidence* with the being discovered—both of them susceptible of an indefinite investigation, but in part opaque and resistant to reason.[2] It is here that the act of faith takes its place, and consequently it belongs to a sphere which is obscure and baffling to pure reason; the universe of persons is one which love alone can truly penetrate.

But we have not yet dealt with the real cause of obscurity in faith. Faith is obscure because it is the revelation of a *divine* person through a *human* testimony. This time, the barrier is quite impenetrable. A human person, while remaining veiled, reveals himself through his testimony—his presence and action—by signs which are homogeneous and adequate. But through a human testimony, a Divine Person can only be for ever

[1] Cf. especially *Vom Ewigen im Menschen* (Leipzig, 1921).
[2] Cf. Delaye, *Semaine sociale de Clermont* (1937), p. 182. This is, in a sense, true of all existence; on this point see thesis by G. Rabeau, *Le Jugement d'existence* (Vrin, 1938), Chap. X.

plunged in darkness—'Hidden under the veil of faith and as if enveloped in a cloud'.

Granted that testimony does reveal this Divine Person and that it is our only source of light,[1] it nevertheless reveals God as hidden, and therefore in so far as our reason is concerned as absent: 'argumentum non apparentium'. As long as testimony remains, we shall not *see* God; the human elements of testimony will always form an insurmountable barrier between us and him.[2] The 'sign' is thus both rich and poor, since it hides God at the same time as it reveals him. Because the Divine Person only reveals himself under a veil, we must say that, in relation to the purely rational order, the act of faith is alien and transcendent: 'Faith is not of the order of evidence, since it is foreign to that order, which it surpasses, and is exterior to that category which is on an infinitely inferior level: almost as an angel is unextended, not in the sense that it has the width of an invisible point, but because it has no intrinsic relation whatever to the category of the extended.'[3]

[1] It is in this sense that St Bonaventure says: 'Faith is called the shadow of contemplation face to face with eternity; a shadow which nevertheless brings more light than obscurity.'

[2] On this 'insufficiency' of testimony, cf. 3 *Sent.*, d.24, a.3, sol.2.

[3] M. de la Taille, '*L'Oraison contemplative*' (Beauchesne, 1921), p. 27.

We must note also another shade of darkness to be added to this obscurity. The person who is born to faith is a *fallen* person. He is no longer orientated towards God as he should be. He is wounded in his intellect and his will. The concepts and affirmations which he employs are on this account dimmed by an opaque shadow; they are 'carnal', and he only succeeds in making them transparent and 'significant' as they should be, at the price of a painful purification. Our faith is thus a 'quest for an absent God', a quest of which the first man in Paradise had no experience.[1] Here again a deliverance is necessary, a deliverance that will take place only in so far as the spiritual being is purified under the action of the Spirit. This obscurity is 'accidental', but normal, and serves as a trial and a test. Putting all this together, we see how St Augustine could speak not only of the eyes of faith, which see in the light, but also of the 'hands of faith', which hold on to Someone in the night.[2]

The certitude of faith is explained quite naturally from the same standpoint. Although the

---

[1] *Summa Theol.*, 11a 11ae, q.ii, a.3: 'So that they sought an absent God as we seek him', and ad.2: 'There was no darkness of sin or punishment in the original state of man and the angels, but there was a certain natural obscurity in the human and angelic intellect. . . .' Cf. *Summa Theol.*, 1a, q.xciv and ad.3.

[2] *In Ioannem.*, Tr. XLVIII (P.L., XXXV, 1745).

problem is baffling on the abstract level, on the concrete and personal level it is quite clear. In a paradoxical formula, scholastic theology tells us that: 'Faith derives its certitude from outside the properly intellectual order, in the order of factors pertaining to the will.'[1] This need be no stumbling block; by certitude is meant objective evidence and firmness of assent: I am *sure* of possessing what is true, because I *see* it. Faith is certain, and thus I am sure of possessing what is true; yet I do not see it. Why then am I sure? Because I am united to Someone who sees. Faith is certain, not because it comprises the *evidence of a thing seen*, but because it is the *assent to a Person who sees.*

This is just what we would expect. If the essential in faith is not primarily the fragmentary truths, but the person to whom we tend through these truths—'Him to whose word we assent',—it is quite clear that our certitude will be based on this Person. For it is this Person, and he alone, who sees the truths, and who can therefore give our knowledge a solid foundation. As St Thomas puts it in an extremely precise formula: the full affirmation does not proceed from the vision of the believer, but from the vision of Him in Whom one believes, *non procedit ex visione credentis, sed a visione*

---

[1] 3 *Sent.*, d.25, q.2, a.3, sol.1, ad.2.

ejus cui creditur,[1] Faith is an assent to the First Truth, that is to an Infallible Person.

The certitude of faith will consequently be inferior in its evidence to other forms of certitude; but it will be superior to them in 'firmness'—that is to say it will be superior to them in so far as 'certitude' implies assuredness in the possession of the truth coupled with fullness of assent. In effect, I affirm intellectual objects which are supernatural mysteries, and which are resolved in the very mystery of the one God in three Persons. Faced with this object, which is totally beyond me, and which God alone can apprehend naturally, the greatest possible guarantee is the word of Him who sees, and this is especially true when it is transmitted to me by that very Person who sees: 'My words are what I have learned in the house of my father' (John viii, 38). In this matter, 'hearing is more certain than sight', because he who speaks to me is the Infallible Person, and I am more certain of what God tells me than I am of the truths which my reason can see for itself.[2] But, looked at in this way, does not the

[1] *Summa Theol.*, 1a, q.xii, a.13, ad.3; cf. *Contra Gent*, 111, 154, *init.*

[2] 'Other things being equal, sight is more certain than hearing; but if (the authority of) the person from whom we hear greatly surpasses that of the seer's sight, hearing is more certain than sight . . . and much more is a man certain about what he hears from God who cannot be

problem of credibility become particularly difficult
to resolve? Credibility[1] is after all a property
of the object of faith as such; it is that character
which the object of faith possesses of making itself
recognised and accepted by the reason, as a
matter of obligation; and how can we explain it
from this 'personalist' standpoint? Our own belief
is that, far from making the problem more difficult, this 'personalist' point of view permits us
thoroughly to resolve the problem of credibility.

Let us first remember that this problem can be
posed on two levels: on the psychological and
concrete level of direct knowledge, and on the
logical and abstract level of reflexive knowledge.
In other words, credibility is sometimes a problem
of perception and sometimes a problem of veri-
fication; sometimes a problem of life and sometimes a problem of knowledge.[2] We believe that
many of the difficulties arise from a confusion of

---

deceived, than about what he sees with his own reason
which can be mistaken.' *Summa Theol.*, 11a 11ae, q.iv, a.8,
ad.2.

[1] We take the word in its full and traditional sense: the
fact that the object of faith *can and ought* to be believed.
Concerning the 'evident credibility' of faith, of which the
Vatican Council speaks, Mgr. Meurin explained that 'the
schema declares simply that it is evident that we *can and
ought* to believe'. Quoted in the *Dictionnaire de Théologie
Catholique*, art. FOI, col. 218.

[2] We have explained our views on this point with reference
to miracles in *Revue Apologetique*, May 1935, p. 538 et seq.

these two levels; for the moment we will consider the first of the two.

If the essential object of faith is a person, then credibility (on the concrete level) is not primarily, nor simply, *a property of an object*, because this object is unique, and because this expression, although perfectly accurate, risks losing sight of its proper characteristic. We must say that credibility is *the property of a testimony*, and consequently *not the evidence of an idea, but the manifestation of a person*. The proper rôle of signs is to show me that it is really God who speaks and that, in consequence, I can and I ought to believe. It is to make me grasp, by means of his testimony, the presence and the action of a person. This is why, in the presence of testimony, the subject finds that it is his whole spiritual attitude which is involved. Credibility is not really separable from testimony. But testimony being the action and the engagement of a person, its comprehension demands an effort of the whole person; being a supernatural call, its full comprehension demands an attention and a desire uplifted by grace. In other words, to speak of credibility does not mean, in the first place, that the object of faith can and ought to be believed in itself and in the abstract; it means first of all—and the formula of Mgr. Meurin quoted above is excellent—that we ourselves can and ought to believe in the testimony of God.

It follows that, in so far as a man does not see faith as a personal problem, he is unable to understand credibility. In so far as he is not an open and desiring soul, credibility for him concerns purely and simply one object among others, and one which does not affect him personally—a pure 'problem'. Where we try to show him signs of a presence, he will see only the logical features of an object situated in another mental universe. Signs will be for him phenomena whose law he cannot find, and consequently they will be incomprehensible. This is not because of their weakness but on account of their nature, which is not to be abstract and general proofs, but to be concrete and personal invitations. They are understood in a manner analogous to that by which the signs of human testimony are understood.[1] In the two cases, it is *an experience of the person* which is in question. St Augustine understood this when he based his study of *credere* and of testimony on our primitive and irreplaceable experience of human persons at the heart of the family, of friendship and of the state.[2] A sign is not understood by connecting it to a general principle by a process of deduction; it is understood by connecting it

[1] Fr. J. Levie has shown this very clearly and has applied it with discernment to the miracles and prophecies related in Scripture in his book: *Sous les yeux de l'incroyant* (Paris-Brussels, 1946).

[2] *De Fide rerum quae non videntur*, n. 1–4 (P.L., XL, 171–74).

with the Person who creates and uses it, with Him who reveals himself and offers himself through it.

Thus, in the process which leads to faith and which sustains faith, the essential is this *personal quest*, this orientation of a person towards a good which can only be another person, this desire for a beatifying truth which can only be a person in whom light and love shine forth. If the soul comes gradually to interpret these signs and understand the words, if it assents more and more fully to the truths proposed, this is because through these signs, these words and these truths, it seeks and it discovers a person who calls it and to whom it replies.[1]

We *seek* a person; that is what accounts for our perception of credibility; we *meet* with a person— that explains the certainty of faith. St Thomas gives us the principle: 'Everyone who believes assents to someone's words; and thus, in any form of belief, it seems that it is *the person to whose words the assent is given*, who is of principal importance and, as it were, the end; while the individual truths through which one assents to that person are secondary.'[2]

[1] This is true even of unformed faith. On this point, cf. the admirable text of St Bonaventure, 3 *Sent.*, d.23, a.2, q.1, concl.: 'By the habit of faith, man's intellect is, in a certain way, rectified. . . . It is endowed with a new strength while it is submitted to the yoke of Christ, to assent to the First Truth for its own sake and above all things.'

[2] *Summa Theol.*, 11a 11ae, q.xi, a.1.

FAITH, A PERSONALISING ACT

IT may perhaps seem that by insisting on the personal character of the act of faith we forget its intellectual character of assent to a truth, and thus lay ourselves open to the rationalist objections against faith. We are not unaware of the danger, and to avoid falling either into irrationalism or into rationalism, we place ourselves on a level which transcends both, because it accepts the exigencies both of intellect and of appetite, and sets them in their right perspective, showing that they are the exigencies of the person himself. This is the standpoint from which to construct the theology of faith as a supernatural affirmation. It is an affirmation, and all the elements, both formal and dynamic, of a human affirmation will have to be found in it. But it is also a supernatural affirmation, whose object, a Person who is Reality itself, will explain the unique characteristics of the act. Moreover, to a greater degree than in other affirmations, this one is a means of possession, or rather of communion, while we wait for that Vision which is communion itself.

Moreover, this would seem to be the proper level on which to conduct our argument against the rationalist, since we are concerned not so much with their detailed and subtle objections as with their whole attitude of hostility and abhorrence towards faith.

The main question is not: How do we justify an intellectual act commanded by an appetite? but rather: How do we make contact with a person? And if a person is reached by an act of communion, can we believe in the call addressed to us by that personal being who is God?

. If rationalism, as its salient tenets show it to us, rejects the problem of the person, or dissolves its reality, it will reject the problem of faith; but even on the human level it will stand condemned. If on the contrary rationalism accepts this experience, then at least we shall have a common starting point. There remains the proper mystery of the act of faith at the heart of this form of knowledge, and this mystery we shall never exhaust; but we shall be able to show that it is indispensable, and doubtless this is the best way of justifying it. Far from putting us at a disadvantage, this *personal* point of view enables us to resolve one of the greatest difficulties of contemporary rationalism, as can be shown by a definite example.

The act of faith is not only a personal act, but also a *personalising* one. It is not an irrational complex, rooted in base impulses to personal happiness and capable of renouncing the hard lights of reason in order to indulge itself. It has its origin

in an enlightened, purified and liberated spiritual
appetite, and it completes the spiritual person
by purifying it and by uniting it to the personal
God. The transition from unbelief to faith
demands a renunciation, and very often a renunciation which would make even the most courageous hesitate. What a sacrifice of our precious
autonomy there is in this detachment from self, in
this opening of the most inviolable 'self' to
Another! What an effort of spiritual purification, of
humility and also of courage is needed to maintain
this faith which is possessed as a living thing. This
is not the place in which to consider this effort in
detail, but we know well that it is a renewed and
deepened gift of the self to the Infinite Being, and
that it always requires lucidity, courage and
fidelity. *The highest human values are immanent in the
act of faith*, and this is why faith is a power of
personalisation. This spiritual effort demands an
intelligible meaning and it has a rational value.
An effort of personalisation which is real, which
brings about a life which is balanced, strong and
fruitful, and which results in the slow creation of
the person by himself, is something which ex-
cludes, in its origin and in its dynamism, whatever is irrational, imaginary and emotional,
morbid and pathological.

It is precisely here that we meet one of the
difficulties complacently raised by contemporary

rationalism. Testimony can only engender an inferior form of conviction, they tell us. Psychological and psychiatrical analyses show that three-quarters of all testimonies are falsified and without value.[1] All knowledge calling itself superior which would depend on such forms of transmission of the truth could only be a more or less refined manner of illusion. Brunschvicg, for example, says that mental pathology has definitely discredited Christian faith by showing it to be a confused and primitive form of belief, since it is based on testimony.

We have no reason to fear this new problem.[2] It will suffice to note that at the heart of this reality which we call testimony, there is a distinction to be drawn. There is a *pathological or inferior* testimony, whose sources are debased, and which is above all the assertion of a phenomenon; but

[1] Cf. Dupré, *Pathologie de l'imagination et de l'émotivité* (Payot, 1925), in which will be found studies on mythomania (especially pp. 7 and 24) and on testimony (especially pp. 215–28); Achille-Delmas in *Études carmélitaines* (April 1937), pp. 27–54; Achille-Delmas himself groups the causes of 'alternation' into physio-pathological, psychological and technical.

[2] In order to clear this up, it would evidently be necessary —again taking up the most traditional views, and making use of the most recent analyses—to build up a coherent study of testimony. A most interesting sketch by J. Guitton can be read in the *Bulletin J. Lotte* (June 1937), pp. 45–71. Cf. also the same author's *Le Problème de Jésus* and *Les fondements du témoignage chrétien* (Aix-en-Provence, 1948).

there is also a *normal or superior* testimony which is not a simple assertion, but an *act*—it is precisely the engagement of a person in the service of a transcendent ideal, such as Truth, Justice, Love or Patriotism.

The criterion of differentiation is, then, this spiritual engagement, with the very high values which it demands, involves and reveals. This is so true that the psychiatrists themselves take account of it, and Dupré, wishing to show the foundation for the (pathological) diagnosis of mythomania, writes these very significant lines: mythomania, 'a congenital form of psychical infantilism, results primarily from the lack of a sufficient curb on the imaginative activity—a curb *normally constituted by the intellectual critique, the moral sense and voluntary inhibition.* It is, then, the result of the development of this psychopathological tendency, or the association of this morbid activity with other psychical defects equally congenital (vanity, malignancy, perversity), and lastly of the setting in action, by vicious appetites and instincts, of the *psychism*, abnormal from the start.' [1] Certainly, he is here dealing with a *criterion of totality*; but we know that psychologists and psychiatrists will look increasingly in this direction for the characteristic of the

[1] Op. cit., 53–54. Italics are ours. And Achille-Delmas, op. cit., pp. 52–53.

psychical life (it is made up of 'structures'), as well as for the criterion to distinguish between the normal and the pathological.[1]

The important distinction, therefore, is between *acts which personalise* and *acts which depersonalise*. Now, the act of faith, considered as a concrete whole, is the very type of those acts which insist upon and increase the value of the spiritual being. It is the act which completes the created person, by the free gift of self to the Infallible and Beatifying Person. If we reflect that it is based on a testimony—that of Christ—which is itself a spiritual commitment, i.e. which consists in this spiritual commitment to God, and that it brings with it a new testimony, because this spiritual commitment affects the whole life, then we shall grant without difficulty that we are here in a spiritual region far removed from that to which puerile, vulgar or pathological testimonies would bring us. *Sani sunt in fide:* faith in fact requires a personal robustness adequate to overcome the hasty and crude confusions of rationalism.

[1] For example, a collection of very frank testimonials on this point can be found in *Études carmélitaines* for October 1937. Cf. Dr Rouart, pp. 102–104 and 188–89; Allers, pp. 133–34, etc.

III

THE WORLD OF FAITH

If the act of faith is essentially a personal act, this should provide a solution to the usual problems of faith. We should like briefly to glance at three of these problems: the starting point, the development, and the transmission of faith—the problems of the unbeliever, the mystic and the witness.

THE UNBELIEVER AND THE
STARTING POINT OF FAITH

THE first question is that of the remote starting point of faith, of the minimum necessary for salvation. We envisage here the extreme case, that of the unbeliever whom the Gospel has not reached.[1] We know the famous formula which sets out the minimum rigorously indispensable for an act of saving faith: to believe that God exists, and that he rewards those who seek him. This minimum is sufficient, because it contains all the truths that it is essential to believe. This has been thoroughly established after years of study, and offers no difficulty; but if we keep ourselves to the realist point of view which we share with St Paul, we shall say simply: *the indispensable is that which man needs to reach the Person who is his End*—the God of Truth and of Love.[2] Now

[1] We do not intend to settle *all* the problems posed by this difficult case, but to indicate *one* principle of solution.

[2] 'If the act of faith is necessary for salvation, this is because, on the level of intention, it directs the acts of all the other virtues; this is why each man must possess the minimum of explicit faith which is necessary for him to direct his life toward his last end. It is thus not necessary

this is the case with the formula in question, as has been noted. The Eternal Riches of the Being of God and the temporal economy of salvation, all this is attained by the affirmation that God exists and rewards those who seek him. Consequently contact with God is assured: through the tremendous thing which is implicit in this affirmation, the Reality of God—of the one God in three Persons—is attained, grasped, affirmed. This is so because the affirmation draws its meaning not only from the real, though implicit, content of the concepts affirmed, but even more from the process of thought expressed in these concepts, and from the movement of the soul seeking its beatitude and so initiating this process.

Every judgment is, in fact, a synthesis of representation and affirmation. It includes a representative element viewed in its relation to the First Truth; and no object at all is ever *thought* except in reference to the Absolute. The essential element of judgment is, then, the *meaning*, the *absolute position* and the *commitment*. Now, in the act of faith it is the whole of a man's being which

for salvation that each man should have an explicit knowledge of all the articles of faith . . .' 3 *Sent.*, d.25, q.2, a.1, sol.2. Although this principle was laid down for explicit faith, it is equally valid in the case which we are considering; as soon as the real advance towards the last end is assured, the essential has been acquired.

is engaged or caught up into action—the whole of his being which desires and seeks truth and love. This spiritual plenitude of his being which cannot be expressed in words, concepts or judgments overflows the mere words of the formula, breaks through the explicit meaning, and by a single stroke—as if by contact—attains the real Plenitude (both Christological and Trinitarian) which is held out through the formula. Where a calm philosopher, considering the matter at his ease, would doubtless see nothing but two correct affirmations, the unbeliever who surrenders himself by accepting the grace offered commits himself wholly to an overwhelming Reality, communicates with the Blessed and Saving God, and passes from death to life.

We must go even further. The concepts and formulas which express this commitment in an explicit affirmation can often be extraordinarily poor and inaccurate. For representation and profound affirmation by no means always correspond perfectly; and representation can, in certain cases, only express in a remote, crude or completely 'equivocal' way, the movement towards the Absolute which is the basis of the affirmation.[1] If the divergence between the two

[1] 'In a region more profound than that of the concept, there exist phenomena of knowledge which prepare for and direct the formation of that concept, as psychology has

is quite usual, and sometimes considerable, in
the case of *supernatural judgments* it can become
extreme; and the ultimate reason for this is the
actual state of man, or, more precisely, the crip-
pling effect of original sin. For it is original sin
which has put out of joint man's spiritual and
sentient powers, and made his ordinary means of
knowledge opaque to the spiritual; it has separ-
ated man from the very depths of his own being
and made him a stranger to himself.

---

clearly shown. These are, for example, the schemata, which
were for so long quite unnoticed because it was only the
tractable results of thought, that is to say the concepts
which were observed, and because no attention was paid
to the rules which governed the elaboration and use of
these concepts. M. Revault d'Allonnes has already partly
explained the mechanism of schematisation, a mechanism
which helps to elaborate those kinds of judgment and
reasoning which are lived rather than thought. Now these
schemata are about mid-way between the concept and profound thought. The solution of a problem, the central idea
of an article to be composed or of a conference to be
thought out: all these are certainly developed in the direction indicated by the schemata, but in themselves they are
connected in the thought at a level which is much lower.
The concept is quite superficial, it is our work which is
already almost detached from us, it is ours rather than ourselves; the schemata is also more ours, since it is identified
with our action; but creative thought, on the other hand,
is less ours than ourselves.' G. Rabeau, *Le Jugement
d'existence* (Vrin, 1938), p. 202. We do not need to insist on
the fact that this is precisely our standpoint on the present
question.

As regards the spiritual, man expresses himself
as well as he can: his ideas do not always correspond to his thought; and when it is a question,
for an unbeliever, of attaining the supernatural
God of Revelation by means of images and concepts made for something quite different, we can
see that there will sometimes be a disproportion—
and a great one at that—between his conceptual
material and his spiritual thought, between what
he represents to himself and what he affirms.
But since he labours here under the consequences
of original sin, it is natural, if we may venture
to say so, that he should enjoy the benefit of his
unfortunate condition. God does not ask of him
what he cannot give; He looks at the heart, at the
spiritual striving which is so much to be preferred
to a stereotyped attitude, at the 'knowing thought'
which is 'true' despite its setting in a false con-
ceptualisation. For three reasons, namely, because the essential of any judgment is not the
representation but the meaning which one at-
taches to it; because the 'supernatural' in a judgment of faith is not the representation but the
meaning—the relation to the First Truth; and,
finally, because the weakness of and obstacles to
the representation are seldom in any way culpable in the unbeliever seeking the truth—for all
these reasons the saving movement of the soul,
initiated by grace, can pass through formulas,

themselves pitifully inadequate, or even glaringly false.

In a remarkable study, Fr. Claeys-Bouaert has shown how one could really affirm God, while denying him on the level of a certain conceptual formulation:[1] an analogous paradox is possible for the act of faith of an unbeliever. There must always be assent to the existence of a God who rewards; but once there is a real movement of the mind towards God the rewarder, then there is a sufficient vehicle for faith: *actus credentis non terminatur ad enuntiabile, sed ad rem.*[2] In the extreme

[1] *Nouvelle Revue théologique* (1921): Tous les athées sont-ils coupables? pp. 179–81. This is no new problem. Long ago theologians explained how one could really affirm God by means of partially erroneous concepts. Cf. Lugo, *De Fide*, disp. viii, sect. 2, n. 23–24, where he shows that in the case of false preaching, 'apart from what the mind conceives on the subject, and apart from what it conceives concerning what is said about the subject; relative to the subject in itself, it is in fact the true God whom the mind conceives. . . .' Also Cajetan IIa IIae, ii, 2, n.2 says the same thing when it concerns God, 'from our point of view, that is to say according to the representation which we have of him'.

[2] Cf. L. Richard, *Le Dogme de la Rédemption* (Bloud et Gay B.C.S.R.), 1932, pp. 217–22. '. . . It is in no way necessary in order that supernatural faith should arise and remain in a soul, for this faith, which implies true thought, to be expressed in correct language', etc. Maritain has taken up this point of view in *True Humanism* (Geoffrey Bles, The Centenary Press, 1938); we may perhaps be permitted to quote here the relevant passage: 'The speculative refusal of God as a final end and as the supreme rule of human life does

case, which is what we envisage, the formula of belief must contain the minumum content necessary for grasping the spiritual Reality. But this minimum which will suffice for direct (and not reflexive) thought, knowing (and not realised) thought, as also for spontaneous love, to attain the two essential truths or rather God himself through these truths, this minimum in each concrete personal instance can only be known to God himself; 'I say to you that many shall come from the east and the west, and shall sit down with Abraham and Isaac and Jacob in the Kingdom of Heaven . . .' (Matt. viii. 11).

---

not necessarily imply, for a mind so blinded, a practical refusal to order one's life with regard to that same God, whose name is no longer known. . . . Under many names, names which are not that of God, in ways only known to God, the interior act of a soul's thought can be directed towards a reality which in fact truly may be God. For, as a result of our spiritual weakness, there can easily be a discordance between what in reality we believe and the ideas in which we express to ourselves what we believe, and take cognisance of our beliefs. To every soul . . ., even one reared in atheism, grace offers as an object, as something to be loved above all things, under whatever name the soul describes such an end to itself,—but it is then a case . . . of its thinking under that name of *something other* than it signifies, of going beyond the false name,—offers that Reality of absolute goodness, which merits all our love and is able to save our life.' (pp. 56–57.)

THE MYSTICAL PLANE AND
SUMMIT OF FAITH

AT the opposite extreme to that just considered,
mystical knowledge is seen as a knowledge of
faith which is more and more personal and personalising. Here we come up against a number of
difficult problems, and we are far from claiming
to have solved them. All we shall do is, with the
aid of theological data and the essential texts of
the mystics, propose a line of interpretation which
we believe to have a solid foundation.

If we examine mystical knowledge from the
strictly *theological* point of view, we shall see that it
comes about as the result of an increasing
domination by the Holy Spirit. Now the proper
rôle of the Holy Spirit in Christian life—corres-
ponding to His place in the life of the Trinity—is
to be *He who brings to completion*; and it is thus
that Our Lord promised Him to us in the dis-
course after the Last Supper. The Spirit will then
complete the Christian personality. And if it is
true that a personality blossoms out by knowledge of itself, possession of itself and the gift of
itself, the proper rôle of the Spirit will then be
to realise this development.

It is in fact through Him that we become aware
of our being of grace, and of our Christian person-

ality (1 Cor. ii. 10–16); it is through Him that, in spite of the powers of the flesh, we are able to free ourselves and possess ourselves (Rom. vii and viii); and lastly it is through Him, the living and personal Love of Father and Son, that we give ourselves to God in charity (Rom. v. 5).

Consequently, it is the humble and courageous docility to the Spirit—*Paraclitum qui nos aptaret Deo*[1]—that the spiritual personality will be formed, and the whole passive aspect of the life of faith finds here its essential explanation. Tradition, we know, is hesitant and divergent on the classification and the rôle of the gifts which are concerned here, but it is decisive on this precise and essential point—that there is no full Christian life outside an ever-increasing total domination by the Spirit and a more and more profound docility to this Spirit. This mastery and this docility bring with them a certain number of essential effects which are strongly emphasised: spiritual discernment, penetration into the divine mystery, yearning for God, and complete liberty. 'It is the Spirit who lifts up hearts, takes the weak by the hand, and makes perfect those who are progressing.'[2] In short, it is He who, in making us truly images of Jesus Christ, makes us truly persons.

[1] St Irenaeus, *Adv. Haer*, III, 17 (P.G., VII, 929).
[2] St Basil, *De Spir. Sancto*, 23 (P.G., XXXII, 109).

Now faith is one of the essential elements on which this work of the Spirit is brought to bear.[1] If it is truly the meeting of two persons, the rôle of the Spirit will be to make this meeting more profound, this union deeper, by making faith more and more master of the soul, by making that soul possess God more and more fully, and by transforming this faith into a power which tends ceaselessly to become more a sight, a contact, and a yearning for God, in accordance with the three factors: intellect, will and grace. Whatever may be the theological divergencies on the exact rôle of the gifts which make faith perfect and whatever may be the difficulty of making these gifts 'explain' the different states of prayer, it remains true that the work of the Spirit has for its aim to make of us true persons by making us true sons—'we have received the spirit of sonship'— and leading us to that Christian liberty which necessarily presupposes light and love. Consequently, if a mystical knowledge exists, it will be more than ever a personal and personalising knowledge.

This can be verified, *on the concrete level*, by the

[1] This point is also emphasised by the classification of the gifts of the Holy Spirit in latin scholastic theology: three gifts perfecting the spiritual attitude (Fear of the Lord, Piety and Fortitude); one perfecting the discernment of self (Counsel) and three perfecting the view of faith (Knowledge, Wisdom and Understanding).

testimony of the mystics themselves. To be brief,
we shall restrict ourselves to some indications
concerning St John of the Cross.[1] Without doubt,
for him mystical knowledge is in no way a knowledge which loses itself in the indeterminate or
which dissolves little by little the spiritual being;
on the contrary, it is knowledge which plunges
further and further into the infinite mystery of
the Divine Persons and radically unifies the
human person.

Its whole setting, to begin with, is extremely
personal. It is concerned strictly with God, the
one God in three Persons, as revelation makes
Him known, and directly with Christ, the 'centre'
of the whole spiritual life. In the mysticism of St
John of the Cross—as with St John and St Paul—
one cannot go further than Christ, because Christ,
understood as He ought to be, is, through his
sacred humanity, the Word in whom we find the
Father and the Spirit; who contains for us all the
divine secrets; and who is *for us* the whole mystery
of God, the Unique Word in whom God is wholly
experienced: 'Since (God) has given us his Son
who is his Word, he has then nothing more to
say of us. He has said everything to us at once,
and in one single stroke, in this Word and has
therefore no more to speak to us. To whomsoever

[1] We shall even pass over the texts of the 'Spiritual
Canticle of the Soul' which are perhaps still more significant.

would ask him for visions and revelations, He would say: "He is my whole word, my whole reply, my whole vision and my whole revelation"; "Hear him, because I have no more faith to reveal to you, nor any more truth to manifest to you"; in short, "there is no other object of faith, nor will there ever be one".' [1] Further, the whole work of transformation is the personal work of God, 'The supernatural workman.' [2] It is God who accomplishes the growing purification and union. St Thomas said: 'God enlightens and attracts by his grace'; and on his level, St John makes use of the same formula. It is God who puts His hand to work by the fire of contemplation; it is He who nourishes the soul by contemplation; it is He who sets it free by purifying it: 'It is God who takes on the task of freeing you from yourselves . . .; It is God who takes you by the hand, who guides you like a blind man in the darkness, towards a destination and along paths of which you are ignorant. . . .' [3] To sum up: 'the same God who desires to enter the soul through union and the transformation of love is He who first invaded the soul and purified it by the light and the warmth of his divine flame'. [4] The attitude of the

[1] *The Ascent of Mount Carmel*, II, Chap. xx.
[2] *The Living Flame of Love*, st.3, v.3, ix.
[3] *The Dark Night of the Soul*, I, ch.iii, ch.xiv; II, ch.xvi.
[4] *The Living Flame of Love*, st.1, v.5.

soul consists in giving itself up to its divine guide: 'God is the principal agent in this work; He alone directs (the soul), like a blind man's guide, and leads it by the hand to where it could not go without Him. . . . The soul, then, must take all care not to place any obstacle to Him who guides it along a path *which he has prepared for it*, the path of perfection in the love of God, according to his law and faith.' [1] And St John will note explicitly that the supreme transformation is the work of the Three Persons in their mysterious Unity.[2]

The *stages* of such an ascent will correspond to a personalisation which is more and more profound. Intellect and will are equally attained and purified by God. In whatever way he uses his sovereign liberty in this process, whether he acts on man's knowledge and love together or separately or differently, he works in no other way than by one single purification, purification of the mind and so of the person itself. We cannot say that there is invariably a purification of the appetite as such; but it is very noteworthy that St John describes its purification as essentially a *unification* and a *concentration*. The appetites no longer disperse into a thousand affections; they all converge towards the centre of the soul, and they 'are concentrated on God as in an embrace

[1] *Ibid.*, st.3, v.3.
[2] *Ibid.*, st.2, *init.* and v.6.

of love'; 'they concentrate their activity and their vigour solely in the service of God'.[1] The more the soul advances, the more it arrives at a profound degree of 'intimate transformation into and concentration in God'.[2] That is to say that the person is unified and perfected in God. It is inevitable that faith—the necessary means of union—should here become 'personal' to an eminent degree.

This it is already, when it first arises in that night where the soul and God meet. We know how the 'Ascent of Mount Carmel' describes this silent and unperceived entry into contemplation. The soul is there 'as one who holds his eyes open with the desire of love',[3] seeking Him whom it loves. In order to unite it to Himself, God will make it go, not beyond the stage of faith, but beyond the stage where the *concepts of faith* seem, to the believer, *to hold the full measure of the reality and the vigour of faith.*

We know that the essential in faith is not the formularies, nor even the separate truths, but the person to whom one tends through these statements and truths. But it can happen that the movement of the soul stops short; that its spiritual movement becomes materialised, that it becomes

---

[1] *The Dark Night of the Soul*, II, ch.ii and xvi; cf. *The Ascent of Mount Carmel*, II, 11.

[2] *The Living Flame of Love*, st.1, v.3.

[3] *Ibid.*, st.3, v.3. This passage has beginners in mind.

set within those ideas in which its faith is em-
bodied, and that it risks forgetting the radical
insufficiency of these created elements, and their
terrible disproportion with the Reality of God.
It is an enormous progress to have traversed the
region of carnal thoughts and to have become
acclimatised to divine thoughts; it is also an
enormous danger to believe that then all is
finished, and that faith is fully developed. Our
ideas do not represent God, and the ideas of faith
represent Him less still than all other ideas, because these ideas of faith concern the personal
mystery of God. From a certain point of view,
they become an obstacle. In their human form,
fixed, hardened and sensual, they are *our* ideas
rather than God's. And moreover, all their individual insufficiencies removed, they are still
only ideas, and so a means of knowledge necessarily limited in range; consequently, they are
barriers for the soul which God calls it to sur-
mount. The task which is necessary is a subjective
purification—of these 'impure' ideas; and an
objective purification—of these human 'ideas':
'as long as one understands distinctly, progress is
impossible'.[1] These distinct forms of knowledge,
these steps of a ladder which bear no resemblance
to the summit,[2] must be surpassed in order that

[1] *Ibid.*, st.3, v.3.
[2] *The Ascent of Mount Carmel*, II, 11.

the Incomprehensible God may be possessed more profoundly. Entry upon this general and obscure knowledge is the condition of this progress.

For it is not a question of entering into a state of reverie, or of a drowsiness where 'one thinks of nothing, one desires nothing, and one does not want to think of anything'.[1] It is a matter of being united truly to God and of really meeting Someone. The surest sign of contemplation is precisely 'knowledge and loving attention' to God: 'The soul is pleased to find itself alone with God, *to look at Him with love*, without occupying itself with any particular consideration'[2]—a phrase which expresses the whole paradox of contemplation, truths giving place to the Person, in a degree never before attained.

Little by little, and obscurely, a 'general' knowledge enters the soul, 'general' not because it is vague on the level of notions and concepts, but because it is a communion on a level which is no longer notional: it is the 'knowledge and presence' of God.[3] It brings into action the pure 'spiritual powers'—those we call intuition and communion. The reason remains empty, deprived of 'intelligible forms', before an 'object' which is more obscure than ever.[4] But the spirit communes with

---

[1] *The Ascent of Mount Carmel*, II, 11.   [2] *Ibid.*, II, 11.
[3] *Ibid.*, II, 12.   [4] *Ibid.*, II, 12.

God, the spirit which is nothing more than a movement of loving and gracious attention, for 'it is passively then that God communicates himself, like someone who has his eyes open sees light passively'.[1]

This communication simplifies and purifies the soul; it makes it more *like unto God*, who is 'without relation to particular forms and images'.[2] This likeness permits and realises the union between the soul and God.[3] Thus, this *general knowledge* is in reality an *experience of the Person;* and because it is that so utterly, it causes the gradual breakdown of the images and concepts which would hold up the movement of faith. With the unbeliever, this movement can raise the person up to God despite concepts which are inadequate, clumsy or partially erroneous. In the case of the 'average' Christian—if we may be pardoned this frightful word—the movement and the conceptual representation sustain and fortify each other; a certain reassuring—and 'average'—equilibrium tends to be set up. With the mystic in the night of the soul, the representative element of faith is seen to be wholly inadequate—an experience fraught with anguish; gradually this element is discarded and transcended, while the spiritual movement is purified, fortified, divinised. For, in the night, the Beloved unites himself to

[1] *Ibid.*, II, 13.   [2] *Ibid.*, II, 14.   [3] *Ibid.*, II, 14.

the soul in a wonderfully personal embrace, 'as if
no other soul in the world were the object of his
gifts'.[1]

At the final consummation, this personal character of faith becomes even more accentuated. 'If
anyone loves me, the Holy Trinity (this is how St
John of the Cross translates it) will come to him
and make its abode in him.' The hour has come
when the promise is fully realised. The Trinitarian
intimacy increases. The understanding enlightened by the Son, the will enraptured by the
Spirit, the soul absorbed by the Father, the sweet
burning which is the Spirit, the gentle hand which
is the Father, the delicate touch which is the
Son:—such are the phrases by which St John
expresses the marvellous graces in which the
Three reveal themselves, in the setting of an
action which is unique as the Divine Essence is
unique.[2] 'The communication of Father, Son
and Holy Spirit in the soul is simultaneous, and
the Three are light and fire of love in it.'[3] Sometimes even, this union blossoms out into two
wonderful effects—awakening and aspiration.
The first is an awakening which comes from the
Son, a movement which the Word makes in the
substance of the soul, an embrace by the Spouse

[1] *The Living Flame of Love*, st.2, end.
[2] *Ibid.*, st.1, v.3, and st.2.
[3] *Ibid.*, st.3, v.6.

of the soul in its substance; and through this revelation of an unparalleled richness there appears 'the face of the Word whose graces envelop and reclothe the soul. . . .' As for aspiration, it is the 'aspiration of the Holy Spirit by this awakening of the deep knowledge of the Divinity'; and by it, 'the Holy Spirit fills the soul with goodness and glory', but in a way which is so hidden in God that St John refuses to explain himself on the matter.[1] We know well the difficulties there may be in interpreting these texts,[2] and we confess our personal hesitation to give to any one of these expressions a precise theological meaning— perhaps the task is impossible. But one thing is certain and suffices us for the moment: this is that faith attains, in a wide variety of concrete experiences, a character which is extraordinarily personal. The soul enters into the Trinity; and through veils which become gradually thinner and more luminous, its glance terminates not in an abyss of indistinct light, but in the living Persons, who are, for it, the One God.

[1] *Ibid.*, st.4.

[2] We are here touching on the theological problem of the divine missions. Dogma obliges us to maintain a unity of action of the three Persons. Scripture and Tradition invite us to affirm a special relationship between a particular grace and a particular Person. We know that theologians are not agreed as to the way to construct the synthesis, but one way is closed—that which would sacrifice one or other of the terms.

Consequently, mystical knowledge is the most personalising that there is, and a totally luminous faith brings about the perfection and completion of the person. The *end* of this terrible and transporting experience is, in fact, a union with God as perfect as may be had here below, the *transforming union*. The soul can only reach its perfection when it brings this idea to life within itself, when it responds to this call, thus fully becoming the image of God which it is already in essence. It is faith which, in realising the union, makes this completion real. It makes the soul accomplish what we might call, in language which approximates to that of St John of the Cross, the *experience of centrality*. It carries the soul into its centre, which is God; and even there it makes it penetrate ever deeper. In each stage of love, the soul attains a yet more intimate centre, and by this very fact it advances into the profundity of God;[1] when it loves God with all its powers, it is in its most profound centre—a process which describes the growing interiorisation of its being, in a growing transformation into God; in other words, the growing perfection of the person by its union to the Divine Persons.

Since the person is an image, and his model Christ, it is in Christ that progress takes place here below, until the time comes when 'life in the

[1] *The Living Flame of Love*, st.1, v.3.

flesh, lived in order to attain the *centre of the spirit, which is perfect life in Christ*' [1] is left behind for ever. The soul is then united to its Spouse to the point of forming only one 'being' with Him, of becoming in Him 'God by participation in God', and of doing at the heart of the Divine Persons what the Persons themselves do: 'giving God to God Himself in God'.[2] 'In the next life, this comes about by means of the *lumen gloriae*—the light of glory, and in the present life by means of a totally luminous faith—*por medio de la fe ilustradisima.*'[3] When the soul is thus transformed into a sort of *pure living relation to God,* it has reached its perfection; it has become truly a person, because it has become—in its measure—a perfect image of the subsistent relations which the Divine Persons are; at each moment filled with the gift of God himself and pouring itself out in a total offering,—'acting *exactly* according to the manner in which it has received, and returning to the Giver His own gifts *with all the excellencies proper to the gift itself*'.[4] The human person is now made perfect by its communion in the Divine Persons— 'by means of faith'.

[1] *Ibid.*, st.3, v.2.
[2] *Ibid.*, st.3, vv.5–6.
[3] *Ibid.*, st.3, vv.5–6.
[4] *Ibid.*, st.3, vv.5–6.

THE WITNESS AND TRANSMISSION OF FAITH

THERE remains one last problem: that of the transmission of faith. The problems of the transmission of truth are never susceptible of an easy solution; they vary with the 'kinds' of truth themselves. The transmission of faith is brought about in fact by means of testimony. Here we touch on one of the essential themes of Christian thought. St Paul and St John insisted that faith is based on testimony, and showed what exactly the objective structure of this testimony is:— message, signs and grace. We have now to devote attention to its subjective principle.

A Christian gives testimony in the measure in which he gives himself totally to God and to his task—the 'Truth', the 'Kingdom' and the 'Gospel'. His testimony implies as its root a personal pledge or engagement to the service of the Word of God, and the embodiment of this pledge in his life. Our Lord shows this in his reply to Pilate: 'What I was born for, what I came into the world for, is to bear witness of the truth' (John xviii. 37). His Incarnation, his life among men, and his redemptive death express for our eyes the reality and the plenitude of his pledge: He is the 'great witness' who has given the 'good testimony', because

his existence and his action are the manifestation
of a soul which is *given*—given to the Father and
to men. St Paul for his part expressed this
commitment to God with that vibrating en-
thusiasm so characteristic of him. Since he has
been set aside for the Gospel, he is vowed to the
Word of God; he is the slave and the ambassador
of Christ, he has sacrificed all and like his Master,
will sacrifice his life for the Gospel. His unparalleled faithfulness and his daring, his sufferings
and his charity, his contagious conviction and his
words of fire; all conspire to plant 'God's testimony' firmly among the Gentiles.

This is how faith is transmitted—by a human
testimony in which the testimony of God shines
forth. From the subjective point of view the
essential factor here is the self-giving of the person.
God can, when he wishes, dispense with it;
normally he demands it, and consequently the
transmission of faith, which is based on testimony,
eritis mihi testes, is based on a personal self-giving.
The signs of credibility are not separable from the
first witness, who is Christ. They are not separable
from the permanent witness, which is the Church.
They are—normally—in no way separable from
the personal witness who, on his own account,
has to communicate faith.

Normally, Christian truth must make itself
known through a Christian person; and we can

describe the process by which it comes to be acknowledged. Personal commitment is the very foundation of faith, and is, in fact, faith itself. It tends by its own energy to become purer and more profound, and issues in a full faith, becoming daily more personal and richer in lucidity, reality and efficacy.

The Christian then experiences the power, the life and the joy which God gives him through faith,[1] and naturally, this shines forth in his life. That intense spiritual *élan* which is what self-giving is, raises the entire human material, informs, moulds, orientates and unifies it by its mighty form. It confers on it a significance which becomes more and more marked. Acts and thought, charity and fidelity, reveal a person wholly given to God, wholly animated by God; and thus the action and the presence of God is revealed through this person.[2] Moreover, since

[1] Bonsirven, op. cit., p. 85: 'The supreme good which (John) never tires of mentioning, under different forms, in his epistle, and which he wishes to communicate to his children, is the possession and the consciousness of this divine power immanent in the soul.'

[2] This is the essential *sign* which is proper to the Church in the world. St Gregory the Great considered it explicitly when he wrote on Mark xvi. 16: '*Every day the Holy Church does spiritually what it used then to do through the Apostles.* . . . What do those faithful do, who abandon the worldly words of their old life, sing of the holy mysteries, and tell of the praises and power of their creator in accordance with their

man is in a state of tension and desirous of communion, he will be stirred to the depths of his being when he comes into contact with another wholly given to God. His whole being will be affected by this living testimony; the organic side as well as the spiritual, the body stirred as well as the soul. The self-surrender which is seen and experienced will tend to evoke its like. The rôle of the witness is thus *to realise a presence and to transmit a call: non multa loquimus, sed vivimus.* In his own degree, he is ever sounding the 'call of the Hero'.[1]

---

ability; what do these do except speak with new tongues? Those who take away evil from the hearts of others by their exhortations destroy serpents. . . . Those who, each day, see their neighbour growing weak in what is good and help him as much as they are able, and by their example and acts strengthen the life of those whose own activity is wavering: what are these doing if not laying their hands on the sick so that they may be cured? These miracles are the greater the more spiritual they are; they are the greater inasmuch as it is not bodies but souls which are raised up through them; and you, dear brothers, can accomplish these signs with God's help if you wish to do so' (P.L., LXXVI, 1215–1216). Cf. this echo in the work of a modern theologian:

'Not only in the sacraments and the teaching of the faith is Christ revealed to us and the celestial city unveiled, but in the whole life of the Church, in the life of all our brethren, who are also a Christophany and a means of grace. They, too, are the Lord made visible.' M. J. Congar, *Divided Christendom* (Geoffrey Bles, 1939), p. 67, n.4.

[1] Some profound reflections on this subject by G. Marcel can be found in *Être et Avoir* (Aubier, 1935), pp. 296–319.

The function of witness is so necessary to the Church that it constitutes a definite 'state of life'; it is, too, of such moment to the believer that there is a special sacrament qualifying him for it—namely, Confirmation. In the strict sense of the word, Confirmation is the sacrament of witness; and because this demands the full commitment of the person, Confirmation is the sacrament of Christian manhood or of Christian personality.[1] The spirit is given to us to make us capable of playing our part: He does not inaugurate, he perfects the new man (as a rule); he does not simply deepen from within, he interiorises in order to universalise.[2] He makes the person a *perfect member* so that he may be a *true witness*. Full Christian personality, in view of full Christian testimony,—*this* is the meaning of Confirmation. Faith being an essential power of personalisation,

[1] Each sacramental character—a consecration which creates a power—plays a structural rôle in the ecclesiastical organism. The character of Confirmation qualifies a person precisely for that essential function which is the *professio fidei*, *Summa Theol.*, 11a, q.lxxii, a.2, that testimony born before 'judges' and before the 'world'. But the world is everywhere, and it is always judging us. . . . Thus, there arises a question of which we cannot here treat in itself: that of the completion of the person (and of faith) by its relationship to others.

[2] On this point see the profound pages of de Lubac in *Catholicisme* (Éditions du Cerf, series 'Unam Sanctam', 1938), ch.xi, especially pp. 263–67.

the ultimate ground of testimony, and the true means of Christian conquest—the victory which overcomes the world—for all these reasons the Spirit makes the Christian a person by perfecting his faith, and by adapting him to his task from within.[1] If the Christian is docile and co-operative, the Spirit will make of him a man who sees God, who touches God, and who is carried away to God—and therefore a perfect witness. This is why, when we say that Confirmation is the sacrament of witness, or of Christian personality, we add nothing to its definition but simply bring out the essential point in the statement, that it is the 'sacrament of strength in faith: *Sacramentum fidei roboratae*' (St Bonaventure). Strength of faith, strength of self-giving, strength of testimony—it is all one. Testimony is not primarily a question of *doing*, but of *being*.[2] It manifests the profound

---

[1] *Summa Theol.*, 11a, q.lxii, a.5: 'In Baptism we receive power to do those things which pertain to our own salvation, insofar as we each of us live for ourselves: whereas in Confirmation we receive power to do those things which pertain to the spiritual combat with the enemies of the faith.' We shall not forget that the character of this combat is 'to fight by confessing Christ's name' (*ibid.*, ad.1) and that 'At Confirmation we are anointed with chrism on the forehead *so that we may show publicly that we are Christians*' (*ibid.*, a.9).

[2] Gregory of Nyssa, *De Perfecta christiani forma*: 'Those who profess to be Christians ought first to *be* what that name requires, and so make their lives compatible with their

richness of the person who has given himself. It expresses the sovereign efficacy of a faith which ennobles and transforms the person, because it is itself ennobled and transformed by the Holy Spirit.

---

title' (P.G., XLVI, 256 B). It seems to us that there are few Fathers who have insisted as much as this 'speculative Platonist' on the necessity of witness, and who have tried more than Gregory to establish its nature theologically. (On its *Christian* character, cf. *ibid.*, 277.)

IV

COMPLEMENTARY ASPECTS

COMPLEMENTARY ASPECTS

THIS rather hasty outline does at least show that we may rightly speak of a *personal structure of faith*. In its objective principles, in its internal features, and in its progress from an arduous beginning to a triumphant completion, faith is constituted entirely by personal relations. But this point of view, far from being exclusive, implies complementary aspects which need to be developed if a proper balance is to be kept. We shall show this by emphasising, in this final section, the *'ecclesial'* *character of faith*. For faith in fact leans on the Word of God *transmitted by the Holy Church*, and this simple affirmation is the statement of another profound mystery.[1]

The Word of God—as we have noted above—was given to us in Christ: 'He spoke as a man'. And our faith bears on a whole body of human words, pronounced by Christ, 'repeated' by the Apostles, and gathered together in the Gospel. But this human word is, strictly, *God's word:*

[1] Cf. A. Chavasse, 'Vie ecclésiale et vie personnelle de foi', in *Jeunesse de l'Église 6: L'incroyance des Croyants*, pp. 136–146.

because it comes from God, and because it is a gift of the Father of light; because it reveals God, taking the place of the intuition which is not given to us, and because it tells us what we could not see here below (John i. 18); because it is spoken by God himself, by God made man, by a man who is with the Father and in the Father, who experiences the Divine Life in a light that does not fade, who contemplates God directly by a divinised intellect, and who, consequently, can transmit 'what he has learned in the house of his Father' (John viii. 38) with a certainty, an authority and a power which are all absolute; because lastly, it is spoken by Him Who *is* the Word of God, the eternal, subsistent, personal Word, the source of light and life; the Word made Flesh so that through Him may be seen the Grace and Truth, the very Glory of the Father. This is the mystery of a word which is at one and the same time a spoken word, in human affirmations; a contemplated word, in a vision whence these affirmations spring; a subsistent word, which reveals what it is through what it says and does: Jesus Christ, Word of God.[1]

This mystery has continued existence in the Church. The Apostles preached this word, so that men might believe it and be saved. No doubt they

[1] On all this cf. the excellent work of Fr. L.-M. Dewailly, *Jesus-Christ, Parole de Dieu* (Éditions du Cerf, 1945).

had a fullness of experience which was strictly in-
communicable, because they saw, heard and
touched with their hands the Word of life. But
from this experience they derived the power to
discharge a permanent, necessary and inde-
structible function—that of transmitting the word
of God with absolute authority and fidelity. This
function is continued in the Hierarchy until the
end of time.

Consequently, the Church preaches the spoken
word: she preserves, and sets it forth, explains and
defends it—*Custos et magistra verbi revelati*. She
bases this preaching on the contemplated word,
for the Hierarchy is assisted by the Holy Spirit:
'the Holy Spirit will come upon you, and you will
receive strength from him; you are to be my
witnesses . . . to the ends of the earth' (Acts i. 8);
for living faith, or contemplation, is always present
in the Church—present in her Pastors who are
always primarily the believing Church in order to
be the teaching Church, and present in the saints,
known and unknown, in whom light and love
increase, well-up and overflow into the Body of
Christ. Lastly all this is realised in the Church of
the Eucharist, which as long as our earthly
pilgrimage lasts 'shows forth the death of the
Lord until he come', by making present the eternal
and subsistent Word under the veil of symbols.
Thus there exists, at the core of that reality

which is the Church, the Incarnate Word become Word-Sacrament; the creative Word, principle and root of all catholic unity; the life-giving Word which nourishes contemplation and preaching with its presence, its light and its life. 'As I live because of the Father, . . . so he who eats me will live, in his turn, because of me' (John vi. 58). It is the *Mysterium Corporis* resting on the *Mysterium Verbi*, because it is the same mystery under different signs and in different states.

It is in this sense with its infinite variety of aspects that, for the Catholic, faith of the most personal kind is founded on the word of God transmitted by the Church: faith hears the word in a religious and joyous obedience, contemplates it in a humble and fervent love, incorporates and plunges itself into it, in a union which is a transforming community of life. There is no faith except by acceptance of the word of God: but this acceptance is only realised in full—on the level of intellect, love and life—in the Church of the word of God. This explains that many Protestants come to the Church through being irresistibly drawn by the Eucharist; all the deepest demands of faith are satisfied only when it has finally grasped, through the spoken and contemplated word, the Subsistent Word present under the sacramental veils.

We may add that faith is 'ecclesial' in a strict

sense, because it is realised by entry into the Church, and by remaining in it. Entry into the Church is by Baptism; but to have faith is to ask for Baptism. For Baptism is the act by which Christ, in the Church, associates us in His death and resurrection—in His death to sin and in His resurrection in God. Thus to have faith is to believe not in a distant and purely invisible power of resurrection and life in Christ, but in this power close at hand, expressed in the sacramental rite thanks to which Christ takes hold of us and, rescuing us from the old Adam, makes us members of His Body. So much is this so that salvation through faith is identical with salvation through Baptism and through the Church. 'He who believes and is baptised will be saved.' On the other hand, faith lasts only as long as the will to remain in the Church. It began with assent to the Word of God as set forth by the Church. It continues in exactly the same way—by fidelity to the teaching received, to 'that message which was first brought you' (1 John ii. 24); conformity to the moral and spiritual demands set forth by the Church; obedience to the permanent and normative testimony of the Hierarchy. These are the essential criteria of that true faith which is eternal life in the hearts of believers.

Faith is 'ecclesial', lastly, because it grows by life in the community. It is not something apart,

in a soul closed in on itself, but its seat is the soul
as one of a community, and as it stands in relation
to the whole Mystical Body, because that is the
setting of its life. If 'my real life is the faith I have
in the Son of God, who loved *me*, and gave himself for *me*' (Gal. ii. 20), it will be a life lived in
the Son of God 'who gave himself up on *our* behalf' and 'gave himself up on behalf of the
Church' (Eph. v. 2 and 25). For the Church is the
Body of the Son of God, formed and unified by
the Holy Spirit. All have received the same Spirit,
all drink deep at the same source, all live by the
same light and in the same love. Each one, consequently, grows not only in himself and for himself,
but also within the Body and for it. Since the faith
of each envisages the same object and the same
hope, and is based on the same hierarchical and
mystical word, it is fulfilled in a vital *en-member-
ment* which affects its nature profoundly. 'The
personal act of faith of each is thus linked with that
of all the others; it participates in the knowledge
of the whole Mystical Body';[1] it finds its perfection in the believer rooted in charity, in his
understanding of the mystery of Christ in union
with 'all the saints' (Eph. iii. 18), each helping
the other, an understanding which is a single act
of the soul and leads to its salvation.

[1] J. Huby: *Les Épitres de la captivité* (Beauchesne, Coll
Verbum Salutis, 1935), p. 187.

Furthermore, this community-conscious faith is the activity which builds up the Mystical Body. By its visible witness, direct influence, prayer in secret and a mysterious communion between them, it fosters the growth of the members of Christ. All the members are developed in the same movement towards a single end which is the entry of all into the mystery of Christ, the insertion of all into the unity of Christ, the incorporation of all into the very Being of Christ. When the Christian says to God: 'I believe in you', he does not say it as an isolated unit, shut up in an isolated intimacy with Christ; he says it as a member, says it with all his brethren, by the power of the one Spirit, in the Body of Christ. The whole work of the Spirit—through functions consecrated to the service of the integral energies of faith—aims at 'building up the frame of Christ's body, until we all realise our common unity through faith in the Son of God, and fuller knowledge of him. So we shall reach perfect manhood, that maturity which is proportioned to the completed growth of Christ' (Eph. iv. 13–16).

It is thus an immense spiritual experience which develops within the Church; and perhaps we should add a few words on this delicate matter. We shall leave to one side the problem of the mystical life, which is 'faith emerging in its proper light' and becoming a conscious perception of the presence of God. We intend to restrict ourselves to 'Living Faith' without touching on the problem of 'Lively Faith'.

On this level, and from a Catholic point of view, faith is not an *experience of God*, if this word is understood in its current and empiricist sense[1] of a contact lived, a presence felt, a direct emotion or impression. God can bring this about, when He so desires, at the very dawn of faith but this is not the normal case. Faith is the fruit of a divine grace which makes the soul desire and affirm, know and love the saving God. But this grace is not disclosed or revealed as such; it is not *perceived* but *perceiving*; it is not a reality apprehended, but a power of apprehension. It gives a new heart and new eyes; it enables the soul to glimpse, choose and adhere to its object; it is revealed, not in itself and in its mystery, but in the fruits of its presence, and efficacy of its action. 'He who believes has eternal life', and faith reveals itself in revealing Him who is 'the true God and life eternal'. But this is not an emotion, a feeling or a vision: it is an obscure assent in a radical homage to the First Truth; it is the most spiritual, the most pure and the most mysterious act there is.

Yet we must add that in faith is concentrated

[1] For all which follows, cf. our *Christian Experience*, Sheed & Ward, 1953.

an *entire experience of God*, because it is transforming and uniting from its very birth in a soul. . . . 'The knowledge of faith, if the heart carries through and follows the movement of the eyes, is not only the evoking of the object but *an intimate conversation with Someone, a converse with a welcome Guest, a dialogue with the Beloved.* In faith, there is embryonically centred the whole contemplative and mystic life—in fact a man's entire life of blessed happiness. . . .' [1]

This life is 'in seed'—and what a difference there is between the seed and the fully developed plant! So this experience of God in faith is not something empirical, or some kind of unsettled condition, but something spiritual, a kind of upward soaring movement, in which spiritual acts are primary, spiritual 'feelings' are put in their proper place, which is secondary; and each element in this movement takes its rightful place in the network of relations.

Consequently, the Catholic does not look for a personal experience of the Spirit realised in isolation, but one which shares in that of the Church, and receives therefrom its certainty of truth. The dialogue with the 'Beloved' is guaranteed as to its truth, its strength and its joy, by its absolute

[1] Fr. Motte, 'Théodicée et théologie chez S. Thomas' (*Revue des Sciences philosophiques et théologiques*, pp. 22–23). (The italics are ours.)

fidelity to the hierarchical teaching, the dogmatic decrees, and the demands of morality. Neither does the Catholic look for experience whose own light suffices, but an experience always infinitely mysterious; because here below, as pilgrims still far from the Lord, we do not walk by sight, but by faith:—an experience always clinging to the mystery of Christ the Saviour, and always lived in this permanent Sacramental Body by which He is, across the centuries, always giving Himself; an experience always uplifted by the profound homage which the creature renders to its God *in hope*; because faith does not 'cut us off' on the human plane, and never allows of that certitude which would cause it to escape the dangers resulting from time, the flesh and the world; but because, on the contrary, it always gives glory to God in the luminous darkness, as our Father Abraham (Rom. iv. 20–21) 'who shewed no hesitation or doubt at God's promise, but drew strength from his faith, confessing God's power, fully convinced that God was able to perform what he had promised'.

NOTE ON REFERENCES AND ABBREVIATIONS IN THE TEXT

P.L. and *P.G.* indicate Migne's *Patrologia Latina* and *Patrologia Graeca*, the first figure indicating the volume, and the second the column.

The works of St Thomas are quoted in the usual manner, i.e. the *Summa Theologiae* is quoted *Summa Theol.*, followed by figures indicating the volume, question and article: 1a = the first part; 1a 11ae = the first volume of the second part; 11a 11ae = the second volume of the second part; 111a = the third part. These indications are followed by the question (q) the article (a), and occasionally that part of the article which deals with a particular objection (ad.1, ad.2 etc.). Thus 11a 11ae, q.7, a.2, ad.1 refers to the 2nd volume of the 2nd part, the 7th question, 2nd article, answer to the first objection.

A new English translation of the *Summa* has recently been published by Burns and Oates. The Latin text can be found in the Leonine edition (Rome, 1882), in which edition the *Commentary* of Cajetan is added to the text. We have quoted this commentary several times in our work.

The *Summa Contra Gentiles* is quoted *Contra Gent.*, followed by the number of the book and chapter.

The *Questiones Disputatae* are quoted by their title—*De Veritate, De Caritate, De Virtutibus in Commune*, with references to the questions, articles and divisions of the article. Cf. the Editions of Marietti of Lethielleux.

St Thomas's *Commentary on the Sentences* is quoted: *Sent.*, the preceding figure indicating the book, the subsequent figures indicating its divisions. (E.g. 3 *Sent.*, d.23, q.2, a.1, sol. 1 = the third book of the Sentences, distinction 23, question 2, article 1, first solution.) Cf. the Latin edition published by Marietti.

In Ioa. refers to the commentary of St Thomas on St John's Gospel. The chapter of the Gospel in question is first indicated, followed by the divisions of the commentary. Cf. Marietti's Edition.